Letters
to My Brothers and Sisters

Living by the Rule of St. Benedict

Denis Huerre, O.S.B.

Sylvester Houédard, O.S.B., *Translator*

A Liturgical Press Book

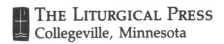

THE LITURGICAL PRESS
Collegeville, Minnesota

Cover design by David Manahan, O.S.B. Cover photo of Abbot Denis Huerre, O.S.B.

Letters to My Brothers and Sisters was originally published in French under the title *Vers Dieu et Vers les Hommes: Un Chemin de Conversion* in 1989 by the Abbaye de Bellefontaine, Bégrolles-en-Mauges (Maine-&-Loire), France, as volume 22 of Via Monastique. Translation assistance after the death of Sylvester Houédard, O.S.B., was given by Madeleine Beaumont (Introduction) and Mary Misrahi (letter of Pentecost 1988).

1   2   3   4   5   6   7   8   9

Library of Congress Cataloging-in-Publication Data

Huerre, Denis.
    [Vers Dieu et vers les hommes. English]
    Letters to my brothers and sisters : living by the rule of St. Benedict /
Denis Huerre ; Sylvester Houédard, translator.
      p.   CM.
    ISBN 0-8146-2241-0
    1. Sacro Speco (Abbey : Subiaco, Italy) 2. Benedictines.
I. Title.
BX2624.S16H8413 1994
248.8'942—dc20   93-32020
                                                  CIP

Contents

Introduction

You will not find in these pages a lesson on the monastic life, how ideally one should live it, or how a superior should redefine it from time to time. This book is concerned with something else: it is a collection of letters sent twice a year—from 1980 to 1988—to the Benedictine communities of the Congregation of Subiaco by their abbot-president, whose function is not primarily to teach (this is the task of each community's abbot or abbess) but rather to support and represent.

Representative Function

Because each Benedictine abbey enjoys full juridical autonomy, expressing and promoting its own singular character, it must be the more careful to avoid that sort of independence which, turning into isolation, would soon cause its stagnation and perhaps its demise. While remaining autonomous, monasteries are grouped into orders (Cistercian, Carthusian, and so forth) or into congregations (Benedictines). These congregations or orders meet regularly in general chapters that focus on clarifying what the order of congregation gives to, and demands of, the monasteries that constitute it. Because these chapters are relatively rare, it falls to the abbot-president (often called prior-general, superior-general, or abbot-general) to act as superior and to represent before the Church and its central government the monasteries of the order or congregation.

Supportive Function

This function, on the other hand, is rendered at a distance, so to speak. This ministry consists in visits made to the communities, letters received, appropriate actions taken, and messages sent. The letters sent to the communities of the Subiaco Congregation are published here.

These letters were sent to some sixty-five monasteries of monks and thirty monasteries of nuns. These latter houses have a different status from the former, since only monks are members of the general chapter and since the monasteries of nuns—which have their own chapters—are called "associated." All of these houses, however, have freely chosen the Subiaco Congregation as the milieu in which to exercise both their autonomy and their mutual dependence.

All of the letters have as their one theme monastic conversion, directly inspired by the conversion of St. Benedict, who has born in Nursia in the mountains of Umbria. Before founding the monastery of Monte Cassino, he had left Rome and gone to Subiaco in order to live there his own monastic conversion, first as a hermit, then as a cenobite and head of a community. As Monte Cassino bespeaks his maturity as a human being and the durability of his work, so Subiaco symbolizes Christian ingenuousness, generous and frail, and felicitously sums up the Christian monastic's ambition: to be converted to the love of God and neighbor.

Straight away, the theme of these letters became obvious: their aim would be to accompany these brothers and sisters in their conversion, pondering with them what can be, in our daily, concrete monastic lives, the meaning of stability, assiduous Bible-reading, worshipful prayer, liturgy, asceticism, beauty, and above all the innate human need to love and be loved.

From the third letter on, almost all subjects touched upon (but obviously not treated in depth) were chosen at the request of brothers or sisters writing from all over the world and asking about conversion of heart, their constant goal and labor.

The differences between a professed monk's or nun's way of life and an ordinary Christian's are quite clear; but more important is the kinship between them. The image of God is inscribed on each of us; there is in each of us a longing for solitude, priceless grace, and flowering of freedom that unfolds in communion with others. In this sense, every person is a hermit and a cenobite (member of a community); and these two words, familiar to St. Benedict's disciples, express the essentials of Christian life that is at once recollection and gift of self, enclosure and openness, in the unceasing back and forth movement of daily events.

And that is the reason (and the excuse) for publishing these letters to monasteries. God willing, they will help the reader to reach out to God, the unique Source of life, and to our fellow human beings.

Denis Huerre, O.S.B.
Abbaye de La Pierre-qui-Vire
August 15, 1989

November 1980

Subiaco: Conversion of the Heart

Dear Brothers and Sisters of the Congregation of Subiaco,

I know the importance of circulating the letters of my predecessors, Dom Gabriel and Dom Maurus. These letters, which were sent to a number of communities of monks and nuns and sometimes to friends—who though not professed members of our order liked to share in its spirituality—have helped their readers to search for God and his kingdom. They have helped to further a better understanding of the significance of what it means to long for, to walk with, to give one's life to—in a single phrase—to live in Christ.

Not wishing to put off this valuable means of contact with the congregation by its presidents, I decided to sit down immediately and send you this first letter with the idea of thinking over with you, who are professed in our monasteries, what seems to me to be the special grace of our Subiaco Congregation.

The wealth of our congregation isn't first and foremost its history, that is, if one calls history that which our predecessors besides ourselves have done with our time, our relationships with other people, and with our natural gifts; or as Christians. This story is valuable like all human history; it is beautified by its successes, by cutbacks, by that inner vigor which prevents and stops monks from taking too much pleasure in the importance of a name or a place, or in the amount of works or gifts which can weigh them down by their excess or by not having them. Because the history of our congregation is totally wrapped up with the period after the French Revolution and the struggles of the nineteenth century and the fortunes of the Roman Church—first during the anticlerical period characteristic of the modern world and other Christians—this history is in itself a lesson not to forget that we can legitimately draw useful direction from for the future welfare of our houses and the Church. The second part of the letter mentions a more specific matter.

However, the grace which is special to our congregation seems to me more fundamental: the point in question is the new style of Christianity lived by St. Benedict at Subiaco.

1

1. Meditation

Whether in the clumsiness of its earlier title or in the more harmonious expression of the new title—the Subiaco Congregation—we are taken back to St. Benedict at Subiaco. By that, what is constantly suggested is the stability of facing a starting point, a beginning, a vital force, which—from the single word "Subiaco"—conjures up not just what Roman history tells us of the reign of Nero or the lake featured in the dialogues of St. Gregory, but that a man named Benedict allowed Christ to work in him in that place, allowed the conversion of his heart. Every conversion can be traced back to early beginnings, and the conversion of Benedict did not begin at Subiaco. But it was at Subiaco that he anticipated by certain acts, and already summed up, a complete lifework: he came back to God.

Listening to the Spirit

Considering Benedict, one can say that the work of conversion does not consist, above all, in ostentatiously carrying out the means of conversion, still less in setting one's self up as an example for others. In the first instance, it is more a matter of hiding and withdrawing into oneself to listen to the Holy Spirit speaking to one's inmost being. This conversion, for those who visit the "places of our name"—I speak of the Sacro Speco—means to love the silent meditation of a cave. Isn't it true that in our monastic churches we have often regained a feeling of preference for their crypts, for the precise reason that they safeguard the silence and that in their emptiness we experience a sense of fullness? There, the loving Jesus recapitulates the most pressing need of the monk, an experience renewed for us at the end of the closing Mass of the General Chapter, when as brothers we stood close together in the crypts of the Sacro Speco and—"omnes in unum"—said everything, in saying to Christ: "Suscipe me."

For if there was for Benedict, in that grotto, a conversion, one can say it wasn't just to the silent meditation and the simple withdrawal from the world that he consecrated himself henceforth—the grottoes and the crypts carry their own illusions—but to Christ. There, Benedict was not just a man a long way from Rome, from his family, and, already—although he was still a youth—from his past. He was, above all, a man who was speaking to God and was listening to him, or, to use the well-known phrase, he was a man of God.

Living in Christ

We have all noticed the contemporary attraction to non-Christian techniques and wisdoms. Perhaps we don't know so well (read the conference given on this subject at the recent congress by Msgr. Rossano, of the Secretariat for non-Christians) that these techniques are not aimed at the void, as we often think, but toward a mysterious presence.

For us, caves, crypts, or deserts possess their beauty only in virtue of the *Name*—(the Name above all names) given to The Presence, Jesus our Savior; and if what is at stake in these places is a struggle, an ascetism, it's not just an ascetism which is purely natural, but one that is engaged in the spirit of Christ, in the depth of his love.

To be wholly in Christ: which of us, professed, hasn't felt the urge for this growth? Benedict, younger and stronger than we, tells us that this desire is not an illusion, for our life is already the very same life of Christ. On this subject, two words of the Rule keep coming back to me, and the beauty of them rings in my ears, not just to express the conversion of Benedict in the cave but to express our real conversion. Without doubt these words, "Noviter veniens," state precisely in the Rule of St. Benedict the moment—which was important for our future—when we were asking to be received into the monastery. Who can forget those moments? Neither the monk nor he who accepts this "Noviter veniens"; for from that time he is counted among the number of the brethren.

But beyond its value as an intimate story, I love a similar expression because it is made from two key words of the New Testament: "novus" and "venire." Each of these makes one reread the Bible, and his attention is drawn first to the one and then to the other. He will probably be amazed at that to which they point, and to the reason for their use together. God is here; he calls. The Christ comes, the Spirit comes, humans come; and then is realized the most unexpected, inexpressible thing: a new humanity, a new world.

"Noviter veniens": that was St. Benedict at Subiaco at the time of his conversion; this was true in our entry into the monastery and continues to be true, on condition that we don't cease to come, and come back again, and desire fervently that change of heart.

Yes, that's the secret of St. Benedict, isn't it? Other lessons can come from other places in his life. Norcia asserts the importance of human and family roots. Monte Cassino states clearly the conditions for monastic maturity and the value of a Rule which has turned out to be more than a list of orders. But Subiaco—that is the moment, the place, and the generosity of the first conversion. I am not thinking of making this grace peculiar to those professed in our congregation of Subiaco. But can one fail to see the opportunity for such a faithful response, felt by us at the same time to be so necessary and so easy, when one recalls the single name of Subiaco? This is at any rate my desire for you and for me at a moment when, without ceasing to be "monachus et frater," I am becoming "Abbas et Praeses." To God who guided the vote of the chapter, and to your prayer, I owe the peace and the simplicity of heart which are mine at this time, and I thank you.

2. Opening Oneself

In the second part of this letter, I would like to consider this matter from another viewpoint. The grace which is special to our congregation is self-evident to those who see its history, but this gift is not easy to put into practice. Let us try to be more specific and draw some conclusion from this. The congregation of Subiaco, like nearly all the other monastic congregations, is international. But ever since its outset, more than a century of communications has borne fruit for those who have taken part in its government. The life of the congregation, indeed, grows at three chapter levels: essentially at the conventual level, then at the provincial level, and in the end at the general level. It would be useless here to recall the ups and downs of this history. Overall, what can be seen to be brittle is, through a difficult path, emerging stronger.

The question, then, is just this: is it enough to have made a start and to carry on as we have done, or can one ask for more, that is to say, have we more mutual understanding and a better effective share of the means at our disposal? The hour seems to be favorable for the very reason that has been clearly stated in the Constitutions, which emphasizes the need to give prime importance to the monasteries and their autonomy; to acknowledge the freedom of provincial chapters to legislate; and to recognize the authority of both the Council of Visitors and the Abbot President. Here is another sign of the times: the good feeling between the Visitors—fruit of their biannual meetings at Rome or in one of our monasteries—is getting stronger all the time.

On this basis we are better able to live out the fact of our multinationality without running the risk of harming the essence of our monastic life by too much centralization. We can exert a mutual reinforcement of our vitality with the help of one another. If we look into this in greater detail, we can see that our monasteries differ in number of professed, in culture, and in actual growth and decline. Here is an opportunity for all of us in the general chapters: those of European chapters which are old but still capable of dynamism, on the one hand; and on the other hand, those chapters of other regions which, in consideration of the promise they show for the future, urgently need cooperation.

I should like the next Council of Visitors to give some time and thought to the value of this matter. I see two ways of studying this: since we have monasteries which are facing difficult political and ecclesiastical situations in their countries—such as those monasteries in South Africa, Central Africa, Asia, Colombia, etc.—how can they help us toward a human and Christian understanding so necessary today? This is the first way. The second consists in pooling our resources. I am not thinking so much of financial concerns, but rather intellectual and spiritual ones that could be realized—and there is nothing very new about this—by lending some brethren for a limited period.

I don't believe this idea is too fanciful, and at the time of writing this letter, the superior of one of our monasteries has supported this inspiration by asking for an elderly monk to come and share in the life of his community, as most of the monks are still very young. The superior wondered if it would be possible to have a monk lent by another province. It is well known that national barriers do not raise the same problems for the younger generation that is able to renew us, that is, those of us who are older and too often scarred by our national contrasts and frictions. I leave this matter for you to think about.

In finishing this letter, I would like to share some of the news of the Curia of Sant'Ambrogio, where I received a welcome by the brethren you know very well: Fr. Giuseppe and Fr. Benoît, both of whom have been looking after your interests for some considerable time. Fr. Benoît de la Chapelle has been here for ten years, and his Fr. Abbot wishes him to return to Landévennec. It was therefore necessary to provide a replacement. Dom Savin Boinot, having decided to resign as Abbot of Tournai, has accepted the proposal that I offered him to fill this vacancy, and has come to live with us in the Curia. Our little group also has Fr. Ildefonso, a professed monk of Praglia, living here for the last six months to help in the house; and Fr. Raffaele Baratta who remains our permanent guest. Soon we shall be welcoming a professed monk from the English province to help with our needs, Fr. Fabian Binyon of Prinknash. Although among our communities we are small in number, the Curia shows no lack of work or joy. It received Cardinal Hume on October 9. It will be happy to welcome you with the same simplicity on your trips to Rome.

The other more recent news: the monastery of Farnborough, which asked for independence at the time of the General Chapter, has been raised to the status of a priory "sui iuris." The election which followed has confirmed the desire of the community to keep their prior, Fr. David Higham. At Tournai, the visitor of the French province has nominated as Prior Administrator Fr. Marie Lamy de la Chapelle. At Pietersburg, unhappily, they have reported the death of Fr. Augustine Van Den Broucke, who was referred by D. Brasò with great warmth after he had praised the remarkable work that Fr. Augustine had done in founding and directing a school of horticulture for the blind.

Since this letter will reach you around Christmas time, let us rejoice together in our rebirth with Christ, to whom can apply in a very real way the title "Noviter Veniens" of the Rule of Monks, the only real human, the human "par excellence," in whom we become human, sons and daughters and sisters and brothers.

In him, our Savior, I give you my "meilleur baiser de paix."

Denis Huerre, *Abbot-president*
Congregation of Subiaco
Sant' Ambrogio, Rome

Pentecost 1981

Conversion and Pentecost

Dear Brothers and Sisters of the Subiaco Congregation,

I shall be very pleased to try to explain the reason why I have chosen to write this letter to our monks and nuns at Pentecost and not at Easter.

If you will bear with me, we shall continue to look at the Benedict of Subiaco and think about the title of the Subiaco Congregation in order to gain a better understanding of the summons it makes like a theme song for our journey together.

1. Easter: Christ Passes Over to God

Subiaco, I was telling you, is where Benedict had his conversion to the single love of Christ, which in turn makes it clearer and more pressing to see how this could lead us to a more permanent conversion.

He Is There, Calling to Me

Subiaco: this is the place and the privileged moment in the life of [Benedict], a human being who on finding that he was loved a little, in return loved to the full and began a total surrender of himself to be in love. At Subiaco, what does this phenomenon of separation provoke? A strong love, the love of a madman, some have said; a human being, Benedict, who seemed to be separated from all that is foreign to love. To love implies putting aside anything that interferes with the possibility of giving oneself, and Benedict leaves all to be completely recollected. Subiaco is just that: Christ worth more than anything else, and the "anything else" appears as nothing. Detachment in such a complete form could not last forever, but that moment was unforgettable and rich in its power to sustain growth.

I hope that each one of you has known what it is like to have these moments. Well then, we can put everything aside very easily, and there isn't really anything hard or difficult to understand about it because we are in love. One can not say that this is an illusion, but quite the opposite: it is a vision of reality. He is there, and he is calling me.

I know there are vocations that are easier to understand than others, and possibly, to some of us, our first conversion may have appeared to be dramatic. For the majority, it was a brief moment, the validity of which is perhaps overlaid with too many explanations that cover up the single and true reason: I shall love you, Lord!

Monastic conversion permits, without doubt, later periods of mending our ways, working away at the task of getting the better of our faults and conquering our vices. But it is the love of Christ that moves one first of all to take the necessary steps very often unforeseen by beginners; and it is to be expected that the novitiate will have difficult periods, the narrow entrance mentioned in the Rule. It is the love of Christ which encourages us to persevere, and permits us to pass on to a more open road.

All the qualities of youth penetrate the Benedict of Subiaco to the very depths of his being; he withdraws from the world, drawing on this power to the full. He has about him an open frankness, and to use an expression that Fr. Congar uses to describe the role of the monk in the Christian Church (and Congar is in my view himself borrowing from Newman), an ingenuity that has nothing childish about it but sees with precision the relative importance of things so that the essentials receive their proper attention.

I Believe in You

At Subiaco one can see faith at work, faith with all it contains. This was all that was allowed for Benedict, and it can be the same for us in our withdrawal from the world and our work of conversion to God's love. For if faith is alive, then it *is* Easter—the feast of the Resurrection in fact—before being a celebration foreseen by the liturgical calendar (but it is possible to forget that—Benedict did). Easter is followed—after the Last Supper on Holy Thursday and the death of Jesus on Good Friday and the long silence on Saturday—by the silence that is so complete yet far from being empty, which accompanies the mysteries of God.

Well then, with the customary channels of communication silenced, our mind—normally eager for knowledge, and our desire—eager for contact and discussion and the need for coming closer together—are for a time suspended. These all have their proper time and place in the life of a Christian, but at the roots of faith something else takes place: the resurrection affects the very depths of my being. There, where I am stripped of everything, the Word speaks to me, and with the whole of my strength I give myself totally to him: I believe in you, Lord!

The direct link between the resurrection of Christ from the dead and the faith of each Christian, explains as well—at least that's what I've often thought—a particular view of our monasteries. This is not something sad and empty, but an austerity that has a gentle quality about it, strong and handsome with a paschal character. There in those walls live the true believers—that's what I've wanted to say when visiting monks and nuns and have been made to look at their less attractive side, at their faults and failings. But in their essential character the monasteries are houses of God where he is sought in faith; that is Easter for me.

These places of silence and faith possess this quality especially during the seasons of Advent and Lent—periods of hope—which prompt me to say this because they are periods of faith sustained with particular strength. These monastic seasons—expressed each day or on each liturgical occasion— begin and end with the Word of God, that is, by the Amen that each one gives to this Word. I should like to say how much I recognize the importance of the role of the abbot and the abbess in the monastic tradition; and I wish to stress this and their need to bring about the life of Christ in their communities through the Word delivered by them on liturgical occasions. It has seemed to me a danger that we might seldom or never say a word about God. This wonderful interchange that brings brothers and sisters the opportunity of help through their need to give the Amen should not be put off because of the human frailty of the instruments used by the Word of God. Our frailty may put off this opportunity through fatigue or fear of some passing crisis, but when God's word is due, it must be allowed to be declared.

2. Pentecost: Gift to Humanity

In either case, I wish to underline the importance of the word said at Easter by each abbot to his community. That is why I have preferred to write this letter to you at Pentecost instead of at Easter. At Pentecost it seems possible to offer a word about our monastic life that may help each one of our monasteries that are vital cells of the great Christian Church. This word from the Father President can reach you like an echo of the Church, and so much the more at Subiaco. In its message, Subiaco gives us an insight on the feast of Pentecost that one might deem essential.

A Man for Everyone

This is the message: More than any of us, Benedict didn't dream to be isolated, neither in his life nor in the Rule. The paschal mystery is not the only mystery, but it shows that the feast of Easter is the beginning—or better—the key to the paschal season. In Pentecost, Easter reaches its fulfillment. The days of Pentecost are days of vision for the Church; then, the novel claim is made that humanity will be assembled without barring anyone.

This claim became the fundamental message of the disciples of Christ the Lord. All became brothers rooted in faith in the person Christ, one for another, one for all the others in the image of Jesus.

Let us look at Benedict at Subiaco: the man withdrawn from the world becoming the man who welcomes all; the perfect host risking the possibility of being snubbed, and even accepting the fact that he might be an awkward person. In Jesus, a unity is formed, and his disciples have a share in this. We can go as far as to say that in Jesus (after his hidden life of thirty years and the three following years) and in Benedict (after three hidden years and for the rest of his life) there was a "Way to all people," directly linked in each case with the way to God.

In the Christian Community

At Subiaco, Benedict made a complete way to all, and this is not a denial of the years spent in solitude; rather it was their fulfillment by a complete stripping that later would be featured in his Abbacy. This we know from the dialogues of St. Gregory. These years would contain for Benedict many harsh experiences which would be very purifying.

What stands out so clearly is the fact that having once and for all left the community of people—or so he thought—he goes out to find them again—this time transformed by faith—in entering the way of the cenobite. We can say with pleasure, using a word that is at hand: the way of the Christian *koinōnia*, the *koinōnia* of the Trinity. We know the rough ways of the common life, and that faith alone—that is to say the total union with the risen Christ—gives stability to our communities. It is this that makes them endure and gives them their Christian significance. We know, as well, the price that must be paid for the kingdom for the existence of these gatherings, where each one knows that he or she must in the future "Honor all people."

Well, this gives us a message direct from Benedict of Subiaco. What is Pentecost if it isn't the day when love takes the form of burning fire and the mutual understanding of the Holy Spirit of God. This is at the very roots of our communities. Benedict has given us his own experience of this, which happened at the most profound moment of his withdrawal from the world: when he discovered that he was speaking with God.

3. Epiphany: Honoring the God-Man

As it is with Pentecost, so it is with the Epiphany of the Lord, another communal feast. One cannot fail to hear the echo of the birth of the Lord and its message to honor all. When one knows the biblical weight attached to the word "honor" when applied to God, one can weigh the burden of the honor made by God to humans. This should become the pattern for our Benedictine way of life: Easter and Pentecost together; a withdrawal from the world in faith and a welcoming of all in Love, compelling us to honor God and his children.

Benedict will legislate later for his disciples. Before this he will take part in their lives, which is the meaning of Subiaco; for daily life is truly taxing.

But do *we* truly love each other? How far? Is it freely given?

Because the human community is always itself tempted by sectarianism, tempted to call the stranger an outsider, and even to dehumanize (a commonplace of all sociologists), what is more urgent, truly, when communities of brothers and sisters offer hospitality, than the need to be human and to give themselves day by day to the task of being ready to take up this aim again? This supposes in each member a degree of true solitude (we could speak of an authentic personality) that has the generosity to give, to obey God, and to do what Christ did.

I will send you each year a letter at the time of Epiphany, and another at Pentecost. Should they bring a word of life that falls into fertile soil, let me be the first to let this word come, not from me, but from where God wants to dwell in me, and where I know myself that I am your brother.

Denis Huerre, *Abbot-president*
Congregation of Subiaco
Sant' Ambrogio, Rome

Excess, Fracture, and "Conversio"

My Dear Sisters and Brothers,

When one of you was driving me to the station, he asked me to explain, in one of these twice-yearly letters, what I meant by "a monk's conversion," a phrase I used when speaking about Benedict's conversion at Subiaco. How can a monk who has already been professed for fifteen years be "converted"?

I could see there was something weighing on my driver, the sort of thing that affects all of us, whether it comes from the load imposed by community problems, the weight of personal difficulties, or the unavoidable burden of life itself. Now the important thing to realize is that until people experience this burden for themselves, they can never understand what *conversio* means. This is why we should never assume something is wrong when we see a monk worried; it can be the sign of a healthy desire to fulfill his promises.

In this letter addressed to all the brothers and sisters of our congregation, I want to reply to my brother who raised the question of what *conversio* can mean to us, but I warn you that I don't have a ready-made answer. This is a subject where I, too, have to feel my way forward. First of all, however, let me say how congenial I find the question, since it deals with what should be the essential concern of a monk, and yet—at the same time— it touches something far wider than our own monastic awareness, since it involves even the smallest corner of the earth in which Christ intends his epiphany to be manifested.

As every community—every one of you—has already reflected on *conversio* many times, we don't have to go over all the obvious points; we can begin by assuming that the Christian life is conversion to God in Christ and in the Spirit, and that conversion is what operates both as purification and as illumination, which are two sides of one reality. By "illumination" I mean what happens when we realize that an *appeal* is being made to us, and when we become aware that we need to make some sort of *response*. In Mark 1:15, the appeal is phrased *metanoeite*, "convert yourselves"; in Matthew 6:6, the appeal comes in the words "enter your *tamieion,* your inner room." "Illumination" also has a wider meaning: what we experience simply by communicating with someone else. When we do that, we enter "into communion" with them whether they already are members of the faithful or are still only potential members. As far as we are concerned, our response as monks to this appeal is what we are trying to live.

There are three aspects of monastic *conversio* that I want to look at:

a. We begin a process in which the rhythm or pace of our progress is always slow.
b. We accept certain "discontinuities" of life.
c. We are led beyond the narrow boundaries of logic and reason.

I shall begin by relating *conversio* (metanoia) to an area where everything seems reasonable and logical—this will cover the first two points. I shall end with the third point and relate *conversio* to things outside that area of reasonableness, where things go beyond what is reasonable and logical.

1. Benedict Within the Bounds of Reason

a. The Slow Rhythm of Monastic "Conversio"

Leaving aside that crucial moment of fundamental importance when we made our first decision, let us consider a brother or sister at the start of the novitiate. This is the official "entry into the way of conversion," and it is here that the slowness starts.

As I don't want the word "slowness" to suggest that I am talking about something we ought to try to avoid, I had better explain what I mean. The point at which we begin to take stock of ourselves in a new way is one that we all reach more or less quickly. By our contact with Christ and with the brethren, we soon come to realize that we are not quite what we thought we were before entering the novitiate, and we have no way of knowing just how far we have to go. It often happens that after looking forward to the pace of life slowing down, a novice can be quite astonished to discover what the elements are in a monastic life that do this, even elements as obvious as stability and enclosure. He can be equally astonished at just how many other elements we can continue discovering day after day; for example, our growing familiarity with the Word of God. Yet the Scriptures are a record built up over long slow centuries and are intended to record the mind and will of God, who is the supreme example of patience. Taking them as our spiritual reading, that is, reading them in a spiritual way, we cannot avoid reading them slowly. We have to analyze them, "explain" them. (In Latin, "explicare" means to explain or explicate, to take out the wrinkles or unfold.) We need to understand not only what the Scriptures are saying to us but what they meant to people in other cultures; that the people for whom they were written lived in a world completely different from our own.

To read the Scriptures is to pray, to meditate on a message God gave to a particular people long ago, and which he still gives to the entire human race, a race that through the whole of time since humanity first appeared, constitutes a utopia in which every human being becomes God's friend and confidant.

Also, since a lasting friendship needs to be developed slowly, the monk's friendship with God is one of the elements that contribute most to the slowing down of the rhythm of his life; though this is so only if he has the courage of his convictions. Otherwise, before long, he shall not find the time to read Scripture at all. When the Word of God is allowed to go silent, the monk is cut off from one of the chief sources through which God lives his divine life in us. Only by slowness can the monk achieve his aim of becoming the fruitful celebrant of a word that he not only has grasped by study, but that actually lives in him.

As monks, we should also look for a similarly slow process in our discovery of the Eucharist. If there was a time when we actually felt joy at receiving it, this was probably followed by a period when the Eucharist became an intellectual problem or just one more external observance. This is because the Eucharist will always be an event where the slowness of passing centuries comes up against the urging of God's kingdom; yet it is in such a simple, stark, and immediate way that this kingdom can be as invisible to someone whose mind is filled with Eucharist theology as to someone who can barely see anything beyond the ritual and finds it meaningless and totally unrelated to life. To Benedict, it was the Eucharist of the Lord's Supper that embraced the most hidden inner depths of monastic *conversio*. For this reason he made it the setting for our profession. But it may take years before we begin to penetrate the mysteries of Christ's sacrifice of thanksgiving.

Our slowness in achieving monastic *conversio* is like the gospel image of a grain of wheat, which illustrates for us how the kingdom of God grows and helps us understand the way each of us develops psychologically. Benedict, at the moment of his own *conversio,* becomes a sudden prodigy of maturity. Yet, for us, the normal course is to mature progressively, and usually quite slowly; and here it should be added that there are no hard and fast standards for measuring this progress. We must use a "slide rule" to gauge the progress of each individual in relation to his particular gifts. This also applies to communities, since it takes time for a group to reach the *conversio* of corporate maturity. Actually, the principle of slow and gradual conversion applies even more to communities, since their maturity is marked by an absence of authoritarianism and by it members gaining the understanding and insight to avoid hangups—or at least gaining the ability to heal wounds they are inflicted. The community that reaches this stage achieves a freedom which allows it to move forward into the future.

This description of spiritual development and its inevitable slowness is what most preserves Benedict's gift to monasticism as he proposed to each individual the task of *seeking* for God and as he gave the abbot in particular the duty of *seeking* first the kingdom of God. We speak similarly today about people who do academic research, people who retire (into their laboratories or libraries) in order, quite simply, to "re-search", i.e., to *seek again*. Politicians, on the other hand, are expected to do the opposite. We expect them to think, of course, but chiefly we expect them to make rapid, effective decisions. I do not want you to think that I would ban decision-making in monasteries—even rapid decision-making—any more than I would ban efficient government; but I do want to emphasize that if monasticism is often seen as a worthwhile example of the truth and beauty in human life, it is due to the element of slowness and research.

There is another sort of slowness that comes from a lack of energy, that takes over when people lose interest; but the slowness I have been speaking of is conscious, controlled, and alive; the steady, unflagging, and painstaking pursuit of the goal (and for the meaning of that goal): the *conversio* of our whole self, the *conversio* of what makes us what we are. Conversion, then, is raising our eyes until we see what we are looking for; the capacity to let ourselves admire without being taken in by appearances; the capacity to love a thousand beauties and a thousand voices, whether we hear and see them in Asia, Africa, or Rome; the capacity of being able to love the murmuring sound of our own little brooks without losing our longing for that *elsewhere* and that *otherwise* which is proclaimed by all that is beautiful, by all that slowly reveals to us the presence of Christ.

b. The Importance of "Discontinuities" in Monastic Life

Life has a strange way of linking slowness with suddenness, of letting its gradual continuity lead to a discontinuity, of making a sudden jump, like spring bursting out after the long, slow season of germination. We have all become used to talking about violence and aggression in our lives, but the abrupt changes which are part of this violence can also be significant moments in our life. Whenever things seem to be falling to pieces, we are going through a phase of destruction that is essential to our growth.

It seems part of the pattern of life that something goes wrong everytime we achieve success; or things come to an end just when we want them to continue. When someone goes away, we talk of "mourning their departure" as though they were dead. But during the war, people continued to hope for friendship and love; they didn't stop looking forward to better times after the war was over, and people behave in the same way during revolutions and can even talk of the future and the coming of peace, liberty, and justice when they are in their death cell waiting to be executed.

Scripture is constantly pointing out that everything comes to an end; and every little crisis in our lives, every crisis in history, is an end to something, a "discontinuity," a parting of the ways, a crossroads—call it what you will—and if some of these changes ought to be avoided, like murder, theft, adultery, and false witness (which are listed by Benedict), there are others that are specifically Christian, like Easter and Pentecost (on which Benedict concentrates), that are just as much disruptions in time, since they dislocate the smooth flow of history and create a new age and begin a new epoch.

This is the sort of fracture that took place in our lives when we entered the novitiate. People who haven't experienced what it means to live that particular moment in the love of Christ always seem to imagine it as some sort of leap into the unknown. Yet, however much that crucial moment in our life was followed by an inevitable, healthy, human, and Christian reaction, the moment itself remains what it always was. Our subsequent disenchantment doesn't rob it of its meaning, but confirms it as having been the right step to take. Without this disenchantment, that critical moment of decision would never have been the first step in our long march. Disenchantment is essential if our fantasy jouney toward a romantic goal is to be converted into real progress toward the true God.

Our moment of entry, of breaking away the old self from the new self, is necessarily a split in our life; but one with an opposite effect from the psychological split that occurs when people are mentally disturbed. Allowing the living Christ to displace self at our inner center is the only logical way we can become our true self, the only rational way we can really be who we really are. We need this break (and not only in theory) in order to get away from the "world of worldliness," from the "worldly" aspect of the world, in order to become the servants of God and the servants of humanity. Worldliness has a way of influencing us at unexpected levels and in unsuspected ways—like the tendency of unmarried men and women to eliminate anything that upsets a smooth life, and to prefer the more congenial ways of doing good by which they remain in control.

For a final example of this break, split, or discontinuity, think of the need some communities have to break away from a set pattern. This always happens when a particular way of life has become so fixed that the members are slaves to a system. They have become shackled in a way that allows them to work but stops them from making progress. One doesn't need to underline the fact that rigid community patterns make it extremely difficult to make a new start.

To sum up: the need for slow progress and for sudden changes in direction are two aspects of *conversio* that can be seen as rational, logical, and reasonable. The Rule balances these very carefully, and this is why Benedict has won so much respect. We can be proud of a tradition that was framed by someone who could show wisdom in dealing with human lives in the delicate area where the divine makes contact with us. This is the side of Benedict that historians and others have emphasized again and again; but there is another and even more important side, one that hardly ever gets mentioned. This is the side of Benedict that expects us to go beyond what is reasonable and logical.

2. Benedict Beyond the Bounds of All Reason

When I speak of going beyond the bounds of what is reasonable and logical, I am actually thinking of a word used by von Balthasar, a word that usually indicates something inordinate, excessive, out of due proportion, the opposite of moderation. Literally, it would mean anything that "exceeds its due measure"; and yet, as von Balthasar pointed out, this word seems to sum up very accurately what St. Paul means when he talks about "folly" or "foolishness," what indeed Scripture means whenever it talks about the extraordinary lengths God is prepared to go in his dealings with us.

By human standards there is something extraordinary in the life of Christ and, however far we are from imitating him, this has to be a fundamental characteristic of Christian life. Christ, after all, lived his life on human terms (even to the point of dying a human death); and to claim, as we do, that his life paid for every sin and moral imperfection, is clearly to make an assertion that goes beyond ordinary reason. Another way of grasping this element of the excessive in Christ's life is to perceive that he was obliged to include within his brief life span every single thing that God needs in order to express himself. In the same way it appears exorbitant that the poverty expected of our own selves before we can start sharing in divine glory must be total and absolute.

Yet this realm of the inordinate is what we are being led to by our *lectio divina,* as well as by our fraternal life. This is, in fact, the reason why every monk needs a second *conversio,* why he needs to go beyond that initial entry into the community when he began his novitiate. It is true that at one point in our lives, acting with God's help—however hard it was to give up possessions and freedom—we did something exceedingly difficult: we gave up our prospects and our whole future. Of course, being human, our response to that call from God was ambiguous; yet, though we do not stop being just as human as we were before, as monks we have an obligation to follow Christ; and that means we must make the same discoveries Christ made, to find out as he did what exactly our Father calls us to.

Jesus was truly human and, as with any authentic and fully human being, his knowledge grew as he made progress toward a deeper and deeper awareness of what his mission was and all that it implied. Plainly, we as monks have the same need to look forward to our common and our individual goals.

Now people, in general, are expected to use ordinary common sense when deciding what has to be done to reach whatever goal they have set for themselves; but what happens when that goal is the salvation of the whole world through loving God in spite of all the wickedness and evil there is? Common sense is faced with something out of proportion, something beyond all reason; and this limitation must be faced if there is to be a second *conversio* of someone who has been a monk for many years.

If I may turn again to my brother who asked the question in the first place: What evidence did either of us give of our folly when he was driving me to the station? Everything was lucid and rational, like the skill he showed in getting through traffic during rush hour in a large city, and (though I *was* only just in time) getting me on the train before it left. Other people are catching trains all the time, so it is perfectly reasonable for a monk to be able to do this. And yet, folly was there, hidden in our hearts: an awareness within each of us of that ultimate mystery of the Lord who revealed himself as the pauper, the one whom von Balthasar calls the first of the prodigal sons. (As a poet remarked, considering how rational von Balthasar is supposed to be, he isn't afraid of putting things boldly.) This pauper, then, this prodigal son, is also the Word of God manifested as silence, appearing as its own absence, as the word that wipes itself out. Isn't it going a bit far to believe that? And yet, that is the faith by which we have all chosen to live. A life (and eventually a death) that, bit by bit, will bring about our conversion and transform us into monks. The way this will happen, the path we shall have to follow before this happens, is something we already know. Benedict speaks not only about renouncing possessions but about renouncing self, which is why this path is called the way of obedience. God only knows how deeply we have thought about this. There was a time when we used to go on and on about how, for a monk, the main obstacle to reaching maturity was an outer, without an interior, obedience. It was an insight that helped us, but we have now reached a stage when it is possible to speak more plainly and accurately about the full maturity a monk is to reach through obedience. In brief, this is attained by following the way Christ himself followed.

Initially, it is important to know that this is a road which has no end—so at least it won't turn out to be a cul-de-sac. It is also a road (perhaps a freeway) on which we can travel at speed. As some of you know, Hebrew doesn't have a single word for "obey": it has two separate words: "listen" and "obey." Scripture uses these as a pair quite frequently, and Benedict begins the Rule with them. *Listening* is something we can do continuously, and it is the way we enter slow *conversio*. *Doing,* however, in this context, excludes anything automatic or mechanical. It refers only to our human acts, that is, actions we carry out with our close attention and with a clear intention. Benedict hints at this when he speaks about the market value of the product of our labor. In this issue, where "doing" is fully human, it provides us with the opportunities we need to accept these breaks in continuity, and means simply that we perform a job until it is finished, and then we are ready to do the next task. When we reach the end of a page, we turn it over. Life is made up of turning metaphorical pages, though most of the time we are not aware of this. When we are aware of our efforts, then we use a little courage, and the amount of courage we need is, in fact, equal to the amount of harm caused by performing jobs automatically, let alone resentfully. As I see it, being conscious of switching from one job to the next is how we find ourselves moving down Benedict's way of slowness.

Finally, we should notice the way Benedict envisages the two parts of obedience (listening and doing), which leads us into the area I have described as "beyond all reason." Benedict clarifies such obedience when he speaks about performing the impossible command. When obedience is carried to this extent, we know we've crossed the boundary of reason.

I wonder if I have succeeded in answering the question or if I have even succeeded in giving a glimpse of the joy that Benedict promises the monk who wants to live, through obedience, in the world of God, the new world, that is both reward and gift?

The Eucharistic Congress of Lourdes took for its theme "The Bread That Is Broken for a New World." As I thought about this theme, I realized that it provides a definition of the monk's life: the bread waiting on the table is the way of slowness; the breaking of the bread is the experience of rupture or discontinuity; being shared is the way—if we allow the breaking to take place—we can enter into the wishes of others and they into ours; the new world is that area across the border of logic; and the consecration is exactly our goal—becoming the place in which the glory of God appears, giving justice, peace, and everlasting life to every being.

Denis Huerre, *Abbot-president*
Congregation of Subiaco
Sant' Ambrogio, Rome

Pentecost 1982

"Lectio Divina" and Monastic "Conversio"

Dear Sisters and Brothers of the Subiaco Congregation:

I am devoting this letter to *lectio divina* in the hope that it will help you penetrate the inner meaning of Pentecost, the feast on which the faithful who worship in the synagogue celebrate, as they once did in the Temple, the gift of Torah—God's Word revealed to Moses, the feast on which we celebrate that gift of fire descending in tongues as the word addressed to all who have ears to hear.

Pentecost is the abolition of Babel and an end to all confusion and separation, the feast of God, who has visited us speaking in the Spirit of his Son, the Word; the feast on which Torah is fulfilled and we become the friends of God; and if it is the feast of turning to God, then it is the feast of our own *conversio* as monks, which is due to the sort of visit God still pays us during *lectio divina,* the sort of visit that converts our *lectio divina* into our own pentecost.

Let me begin with a point on which many of you will agree: *Lectio divina* in the monastic life as we are leading it is going through a serious illness. Turn again, as we did in my last letter, to Benedict's *conversio* when he was a hermit at Subiaco, when so much of his time was spent reading Scripture while cut off from access to any great library. The sort of distinction we used to make between pious reading and *lectio divina* would have been meaningless to him. To read meant to read the Bible and, by converting that reading to prayer, to reach one's own *conversio* which alone turns us into the friends of God.

Reading in the sixth century still involved a movement of the lips and many monks found this helped them to be moved by God in the heart. *Lectio divina* is when we work with God's word so that it may work inside us, transforming our behaviour, our ideas, our life.

How often have we noticed the great similarity between Moses and Benedict? Each on his mountain, "with foot unshod and listening to God in his heart"; each at a distance from the crowds, free to enter the Cloud, the cell, the heart, and free to do nothing but listen.

A letter from one of you says: "Ever since the year began I have been trying to enter into the Gospel of Luke so as to live it. It has made me realize that what was missing from my life as a monk, what I had never noticed, was the effect produced by listening to the Word of God." I quote this as an illustration of the serious attempts being made in all our communities, on all the continents, and in common with all monastic orders, to translate general principles into practical life.

The fact is that in spite of endless conferences and lectures on "Scripture in monastic life," of endless talks on the Bible with audiovisual aids, communities have not been radically changed. So much gets lost in the very process of putting these principles into practice. What is lacking isn't the willingness and courage to do something about it, still less a proper appreciation of liturgy, but the actual practice of true *lectio divina* itself. Without that, monastic life, whether in choir or at work, both mental and manual, will lack the living strength of faith. All abbots, novice masters, lecturers, and preachers must know Scripture, or they risk betraying the Word of God; but this duty, which they can fulfill by studying Scripture, isn't at all what is meant by *lectio divina*.

I have no intention here of going over all we covered in the novitiate about when and how prayer can be labeled *lectio, meditatio, contemplatio*, and *oratio*. All I want to do is to suggest three ways of broadening the vision we have of our life:

1) How life becomes monastic through *lectio divina*;
2) The liberation we reach through *lectio divina*;
3) A few practical conclusions from these two points.

I hope you take what I say as a sincere attempt to meditate on how the Spirit and Word of God penetrate what we are and what we do.

1. The Shape and Framework of Monastic Life and How It Becomes Monastic Through "Lectio Divina"

By the shape or framework of any life, I mean simply its basic rhythm of beginning, maturity, and decline. For Christians, life is both gift and resurrection, two realities that enlarge every succeeding instant as it comes into being and passes away. Life itself is that continuous movement out of the distance now passing away into the distance looming ahead. Seen this way, no single instant in our life is ever isolated, and those who have come to realize this know what it is to feel that island-in-time we call "now" growing and expanding all around us. It is an experience that feels as if we were being carried off by a breath of wind—perhaps like the people Jesus mentions in Luke (16:16) who had been carried away ever since John began preaching the good news of the kingdom—good news which has been spreading ever since, with "everyone getting carried away trying to enter it."

This framework of monastic life, shaped by its own inner rhythm, is not a frame fencing us in like a prison; it is simply the way each of us adapts our personal frontiers and boundaries to coincide with those of our neighbor, that is, contact with others across these frontiers that we achieve by *lectio divina*. And the only alternative is to do without boundaries, to avoid having any shape to our life, and to live in an unreal aloneness, to create—in fact—an artificial solitude in community.

Communal life puts us constantly on the doorsteps of other people, puts us at their disposition, and yet, at the same time, allows us to live in harmony with all the sides of our own character, with all the elements that make up our own personality; and that is a harmony which becomes essential if we want to *call* ourselves the brother of the rest; even more essential if we truly want to *be* their brother, available to them as a full human being. Within such a framework, we are given equal access to real solitude and to authentic communion, to being equally ingoing and outgoing. This is what has always proved to be the unique interest in Benedictine monachism.

The aspect of our Benedictine framework that writers always quote is the allocation of our time to "work, prayer, and reading"; but, thanks to our own selves, it is precisely this which has become petrified: we have succeeded in fossilizing it by our very attempts to make it understood and by our failure to allow for all the nuances we find in Benedict, but which we have wiped out by blindly insisting on each day having so many hours for this and so many for that. On this point, fortunately, all I need do is refer you to Dom Adalbert de Vogüé (*Sources Chrétiennes* 185.593). He says: "Unlike all the other monastic rules written before his death, Benedict seems quite uninterested in sanctifying particular moments of the day according to a precise timetable. He lays down exact rules for the amount of time spent on reading and work, but not for the *opus dei*. In the *Regula Magistri*, reading and work are simply ways of filling in the gaps between divine office; in Benedict, however, they are treated with the respect due to honest jobs that need to be properly done and that require a specific amount of time if we are going to undertake them seriously."

Benedict gives as much thought to the time needed for *lectio divina* as he does to the harm that would be caused by letting it go on too long. Rather than risk it dissipating into daydreams, he is not afraid to fix a limit to the time spent on our search for God. To quote Dom Vogüé again: "The most important thing in the system that had become traditional by the time of Benedict was Divine Service; what was important to Benedict, however, was preserving the rhythm of human life: effort and rest, manual work and spiritual work. And yet, far from this making the profane more important than the divine, Benedict sees every aspect of monastic life as equally sacred. He was unique in refusing to allocate a fixed amount of time to the Office, so unique, in fact, that he has never been copied by any rule written since his death, not even by the rules that claim to be modeled on his.''

But on *lectio divina* (to return to our subject), Benedict, unlike Benedictines today, is intractable. We have good reasons for our customs, our excuses are perfectly valid, and we all have jobs that have to get done: going to choir, earning our living, since we, unlike the lilies ''that labor not,'' are no longer supported by the wealth of others. There is serious and demanding academic study; there are always the guests who need attention; and all the other things that take up just as much time in large communities as in small ones. All this is what creates the problem of how Benedict's ideal can best be harmonized with the modern demands of community structure. In these circumstances, it isn't any wonder that *lectio divina* is the poor relation, neglected by most of us without any qualms of conscience because there always are other things that are always more urgent.

When a problem is created by there always being something that really is more urgent to do, the most urgent thing to be done is to find a solution. The abbot and community of every monastery face this dilemma constantly and I have every sympathy for them; but in this letter, at least, my immediate concern is with the biblical tradition of reading Scripture in a scriptural way, since that is the way we are meant to find God addressing his word to ourselves, and how we find his living, creative word creating the inner liberty which is the only true human life.

2. Life as Liberty; Monastic Life as Reaching Liberation Through ''Lectio Divina''

The way to live so that we are glad to be alive is what Benedict supposes we were all looking for when we entered the monastery, and what God offers us to meet that need is the experience of liberty in Christ. There are some Benedictines who, at least subconsciously, are looking in the monastery for a way of life that will enable them to avoid taking any initiatives, a safe life without any risks; but here I am concerned with the majority— whether among the novices or the professed—whose aim is the perpetual deepening of their inner liberty.

Where there is breath there is life, and our aim is the life we have when we breathe with God's own breath; our growth depends on realizing this. Some people take this to be a paradox, but we are liberated through having the monastic framework in which to live, since it is this that liberates us from egotism. Yet, this isn't something we can experience communally; we find it only in the secret of our private interior life—as indeed we discover from the outset in our *lectio divina*. The whole of Scripture is a poem on liberty, on the lasting safety of everlasting salvation reached through the freedom and liberation that alone makes our life real and keeps it that way.

We can use the term "spiritual reading" to cover all the ways in which we read events as well as books in order to understand what they mean in the light of faith. *Lectio divina,* on the other hand, is a term taken from Benedict, and in this letter I am using it strictly as he used it, to mean the reading of Scripture and those patristic commentaries that go to make up the Patrologia. I am concentrating on this because it is fundamental, which is to say that without Scripture and the patristic way of understanding it, there simply would not be any method of understanding events and books that would justify us calling it "spiritual reading."

The proclamation of God's word in church and *lectio divina* can never be substitutes for each other. For Benedict, *lectio divina* is the way we learn how to listen to the word at our liturgy, where it is proclaimed in the way Scripture is intended to be. This remains true for the extraliturgical groups in some monasteries that meet for Bible readings and *meditatio*. These groups have been improvised to meet a particular need or to supply something that was lacking; but their value does not depend on how far they supply what— through our poverty—we lack, but on how much we can bring to them from our inner abundance and personal riches. Every period in the history of monasticism has been able to produce some new, original contribution to our tradition and, if only to ensure that new developments will always remain possible, we ought not to decry them.

The essential thing for us to consider is what the valid motives are that urge cenobites toward this inner contact with the Word of God, with the aim of hearing what it says to each particular listener. Before we consider this, however, let us remember that far from expecting his word to be listened to from a distance, God puts it in our heart and in our mouth. In Deuteronomy we read (30:12): "You won't have to wait till someone goes up to heaven or crosses the sea in order to find out what I want, and then await his return to tell you, so that you can both know it and do it, for I put my commandment in your mouth and in your heart." When Paul comments on this passage, he says to the Romans (10:6-8): On the one hand, Leviticus tells us (18:5) that those who obey the written word of God will live, and on the other hand, Deuteronomy says we have no need to go to heaven or down to the bottom of the sea to know God's word as it already is in our mouth and our heart. We can either do God's will because Moses tells us what it is, or we can do it because we know it from inside ourselves. The first way is becoming holy through law, the second is becoming holy through faith. In fact, Jesus did descend to the depths and ascend to heaven, from which he had come. Believing this in the heart, we proclaim it with our mouth.

Let me now try to summarize in three points what I see as essential to understanding the motives that lead cenobites to this inner contact with God's word:

a. Covenant and Profession

By our profession, we Benedictines are witnesses to the covenant with God recorded in the Scriptures. We can speak loosely about our profession in the terminology invented to describe primitive initiation rites—a series of steps, beginning with the rule read to the novice and ending with his acceptance as brother by all who make up the community into which he is being initiated. We can speak a little more accurately about profession as being similar to the ceremonies of baptism, which are also a sort of ritual initiation.

A far more accurate way to speak about profession, however, is to compare it to the various covenants which we read about in Scripture between named parties, which list the obligations contracted as well as the sanctions or penalties that follow if the covenant is broken. This leads us to see the most accurate way of talking about profession: by comparing it with the covenant established by Christ in the Eucharist, which is the moment and place designated by Benedict for the profession to be made.

It is obvious that he saw the altar as the only appropriate place for the Benedictine to become a brother; because it was at the Last Supper that Jesus, fulfilling all those earlier covenants, established the New Covenant, the New Testament, and laid down his new commandment (not just of loving each other but of loving each other as he loved us).

There are several English words we can use for this relationship: covenant, contract, alliance, testament, or pact. We can also call it an engagement, and even more, a marriage. This is what makes it appropriate for so many nuns (and some monks) to wear an engagement or wedding ring. Putting on that outer sign of the mystical marriage or covenant is a reminder that, as Benedictines, we put on Christ, who is the true covenant in whom the marriage of human and divine most perfectly exists. For us to carry Christ the covenant is to carry the Ark of the Covenant that enshrines the Word of God. Our document of profession itself is nothing but a summary of God's word enshrined in Scripture.

b. The Patristic or Benedictine Method of "Lectio Divina"

A single theme running through the entire Bible is our need for *conversio*, for turning to God, in spite of all its difficulties and our own incapacities. As Benedictines our life is geared to making us understand this.

When, as Christians, we talk of the "old" *and* "new" testaments or covenants, we should try to realize the depth of meaning contained in that word *and*. The Old Testament records a whole series of testaments or covenants: by calling it *the* Old Testament, we acknowledge that the whole series forms one single covenant, renewed again and again. When we enlarge the series to include the covenant of the New Testament, that series still constitutes one single covenant, its unity being emphasized by the word *and*, a unity that exists in Christ.

It is true that we talk of being a "new creation" in Christ, yet the phrase "New Testament" is actually a term taken from the Old Testament. That being so, how far can we talk of Christ's testament existing before him in the "new testament" to which Jeremiah (31) refers? Is the covenant or testament of Christ called "new" in the sense of being a novelty introduced by him and wholly unknown to the Old Testament? Surely, Christ himself answers that by telling us that he was sent not to innovate but to fulfill. These are deep questions, and the answer to them affects our lives as human beings, as well as our lives as Catholics; it is the same God who makes use of the patriarchs, of the prophets, of Jesus, of ourselves, and of all who proclaim God's word.

As Bernard in his last book asks the question "Who *is* God?", so the Church, as long as it is faithful to Christ, will ask incessantly "Who *is* Jesus?" These are the questions that should be fixed permanently in the seeking mind of a monk. It is probably when we turn to this "seeking" that is done by Benedictines—to this monastic quest—that we discover how important it is to distinguish between the patristic method of finding Christ on every page of the two Testaments, from the first page to the last page of the Bible, and the method described by von Balthasar as "simply comparing the record of Christ who came to fulfill, with the various texts he is supposed to have fulfilled." It is only in accordance with the first or patristic method that Benedict can say that every page of the Bible, every word of God, is a complete and sure guide to the way a human life should be led.

Augustine coined a catchy phrase when he said: "The New Testament is veiled in the Old, and the Old unveiled in the New," but this is no more than a dangerous half-truth. All it does is suggest that, primed by the New Testament, we already know exactly what we are going to find in the Old Testament once we succeed in removing the veil composed of imagery and symbolic language. As von Balthasar says, contemporary exegesis is essential if we are going to take the dialectical theology of salvation at all seriously.

How far should we go to avoid the risk of reading Scripture in a superficial, naive way? Should we allow this risk to be a good excuse for not reading it at all? A better solution is to distinguish between the harmful, fundamentalist Bible reading on the one hand—with its subjective interpretation of the text—and, on the other hand, *lectio divina*, which is not a matter of reading the text but of listening to the Word.

In this way Scripture actually ceases to be a written text and becomes our food: we eat it so as to be nourished on "every word that comes from the mouth of God," on the spiritual bread by which we live as we receive it into our heart. On this basis we can distinguish between a time for study and a time for *lectio divina*, between reading the text and listening to the word addressed to us personally, both as the living word sustaining our life and as the creative word transforming us. And yet, the text before us at the times of study may be the same text before us during *lectio divina:* in the first case we are busy working on the text; but it is the text itself, in the second case, which is working on us.

c. "Lectio Divina" as Therapy

One may have noticed how rare it is for the Jewish people to feel attracted to idolatry, and biblical commentators are surely right when they suggest that this is due to the repeated warnings against it in Scripture. Catholics and Jews, however, share a paradox: precisely where we are protected by the divine laws from all the sins like idolatry to which we are tempted, our religion prepares the trap of tempting us to legalism, which remains today as much a menace as when Jesus warned us against it. And far from escaping it, monks above all find it a daily and perpetual menace.

Against this, the best and safest remedy is *lectio divina*, because the effect it produces—if we let it act on us—is precisely that *puritas cordis* which has always been the specific, scriptural, and monastic cure for legalism. It might help to quote von Rad at this point: "When a particular need gives birth to a regulation, we have a living law upheld by the inner strength of society; when that need has passed, we have a law imposed by external constraint." An excellent description of legalism is provided by Fr. Voillaume who speaks of our attempts "to rationalize the kingdom of God." Happy indeed a monastery where each and all would avoid this snare through *lectio divina;* it would be a true house of listening and searching.

3. Practical Conclusions from the First Two Points: The Pastoral Value of "Lectio Divina"

This is a question I approach with some diffidence, for advice from outside about one's inner life can so easily be resented. So let me say what I feel in three brief points:

a. Extended "Lectio Divina"

Even at Mont-Dieu, William of St. Thierry recommended no more than a set period each day for *lectio divina*. This is the usual custom in all our own monasteries, some of which, however, have experimented with occasional extensions of this period, setting aside a whole day, a whole week, during which every spare moment is devoted to *lectio divina;* not just to reading sacred texts and spiritual books, but to that secret encounter with the Word of God. Some have found the results unexpected, as it brought to the surface the most hidden of our inner longings.

b. A Particular Approach to "Lectio Divina"

More than at any other time, it is during *lectio divina* that we are prone to being disturbed by others, distracted, and even bored. Yet Scripture itself proposes a way of avoiding this. Instead of being a particular solitary human being, engaged in *lectio divina* at a particular time defined by calendar and clock, allow yourself to identify with all the human beings you are reading about: good and bad, Greek or Jew, rich and poor, wise or foolish, publican and Pharisee, with anyone saying either yes or no to God. And do this standing perpetually in the presence of God, leading a lamb with one hand and a wolf with the other, since both are "me" and they must be there together in order to tell God that he is the prince of the peace who exists between them.

As I perceive myself this way in Scripture, my *lectio divina* becomes a sacrifice acceptable to God. It may seem at first a complicated method, but as we read, the word at the center becomes simpler and simpler till it reaches the point where God can be found in it, consecrating the time we have spent as a true pentecost.

This method of *lectio,* suggested by Scripture itself, helps one to accept other humans, to be open to everyone other than oneself. One interpretation of Psalm 60 sees it as a great song of peace in which the cantor is God himself chanting our whole human race into unity under his divine sceptre, which is the Messiah from Jacob. If I refuse to close my door on anyone, if I welcome everyone who happens to come in, then once more my *lectio* becomes a true pentecost.

c. The Fruit of "Lectio Divina"

Who was prepared for the new wine of Pentecost? The unexpected happened then, as it does now, in *lectio divina,* in that encounter—safe from prying eyes—between *the* Word and *my own* word, an encounter that is never far removed from that luminous moment in the dark when Jacob became Israel. Anything can happen during *lectio divina:* the Word becomes our song and our food; circulating in the heart, it becomes our dance; entering what we write, it becomes our toy as it did when captured by the brush of Benedictines who illuminated manuscripts. Freedom of body, freedom of heart, freedom of spirit, all conspire to make *lectio divina* bring us down to earth at the very moment we are traveling with it through outer space. No limits can be set to the freedom we enjoy when celebrating the Word of our Life, and there isn't a monastery, there isn't a nun or monk, who doesn't have access to this liberty.

Lectio divina and Pentecost: two things that fuse together in moments when we can no longer distinguish between what the Spirit is saying to the churches and what the Spirit is saying to us; moments when God hears an echo, in my voice, of the voice of his Messiah.

With every festal greeting for Pentecost,

Denis Huerre, *Abbot-president*
Congregation of Subiaco
Sant' Ambrogio, Rome

Epiphany and Pentecost 1983

Part I: Epiphany 1983

To All Members of the Subiaco Congregation:

In the course of these letters devoted to Benedict at Subiaco, many of you have suggested so many aspects of his conversion (which is our main theme) that this will be the first part only of a double letter, an introduction to the next which will deal with *fuga mundi,* our "flight from the world." This preface to that theme will be devoted to Peter and Paul and to how they relate our *conversio* to the faith of the Gospels. Taken together, the two parts will be an attempt to identify the context in which we carry out our monastic work of *conversio.*

Let me begin with Sant' Ambrogio, not because it is the least typical of all our houses, having only four members who are not always free even to be all in residence at the same time, but because I want to mention the three characteristics of Sant' Ambrogio that suggest how Peter and Paul could be the focus of this introduction to *fuga mundi:*

The first of these three characteristics involves the excavation carried out beneath Sant' Ambrogio in 1982, which uncovered one of the walls of the Portico of Philip. Porticus Philippi was built 27 B.C.E. by Marcius Philippus, the stepfather of Augustus, and designed to surround and honor the Templum Herculis Musarum. This temple was built nearly two hundred years before by Fulvius Nobilior after his victories over the Aetolians, who had broken their treaty with Rome. From this campaign he brought back, among other art treasures, the Aetolian statues of the nine muses. This was the portico built side by side with the Portico of Octavia constructed by Augustus in memory of his sister and endowed with a library and art gallery. These are in the area south of the Flaminian Circus, between it and the Tiber. To the east of this space is the theatre of Marcellus; to the west, the theatre of Balbus.

The second characteristic is a painting we have at Sant' Ambrogio, which has just been photographed by two students from Milan. It shows the Apostles Peter and Paul giving each other the kiss of peace (though some have thought it may depict Peter and Andrew greeting each other).

The third characteristic is the actual location of Sant' Ambrogio in the ghetto organized by Paul IV in 1555, so that even now we are the neighbors of the chief rabbi and located within a few yards of the modern synagogue.

The link between these three characteristics isn't simply their accidental connection with Sant' Ambrogio: Hercules and Roman paganism, the apostolic kiss of peace and Christianity, the synagogue and Israel are all linked to each other within the spiritual area in which our *conversio* takes place. A *conversio* due to the apostolic word being received by a living paganism while uttered from the mystery of that unbreakable union between the Old and New Testaments.

1. Pagans and Christian "Conversio"

There is a direct continuity between the Hebrew prophets attacking idols and idolatry and saints like Benedict destroying pagan temples and statues; yet, after this came the reuse not only of the stones, but also of the spiritual values the pagan idols had enshrined. Whenever we see this process at work, we see it is always as part of a complex development, not just the simple process imagined by those who find it a stumbling block and even assume it to be the work of Satan. In spite of all the centuries spent clarifying Christian ideas about paganism, it is still very helpful to keep in mind the example the apostles give of how to approach the problem. Paganism involves polytheism as well as atheism, and it includes all the many ways in which the natural religious tendency of humans manifests itself in Christians and in others. At many times and in many places, it has constituted a proof of the true nobility of human aspirations, and *that* in spite of anything that stained it. This is directly implied in Christ's claim that he came to fulfill all things, since that includes our natural urge to lead a full life as well as our need to understand it and recognize what it is.

Here we reach the precise point that is the theme of this letter; the pagan milieu in which Christian conversion takes place; the milieu of moral paganism as well as the milieu of our own ignorance, of that ignorance which is so often cited in Scripture and by the Church to account for the paganism from which we are to be converted. Many sayings of Christ refer to this: "they know not what they do"; "they are blind;" etc. As Christians we are meant to know and to see, and yet we are all conscious of our blindnesses and lack of knowledge of awareness, which is to say that we are conscious or our own paganism.

On the other hand, we have to remember that no human being is so ignorant as to be without some inkling or intuition that Truth and Justice are one. This is why Christians and pagans so often find themselves talking at cross purposes when using words like "god" or "the gods." What pagans and Christians do have in common can, of course, be seen in words and gestures that reflect our common humanity; but we see it best when comparing ideas about what humanity is and what it could be like in an ideal future.

Think, for instance, of Hercules (Herakles) even though he was, strictly speaking, a demi-god only. To begin with, being the patron of strength, the personification of divine power, he provides an immediate and obvious symbol of common ground between Christianity and the classical pagan world. It was this aspect of Hercules that led Fulvius Nobilior, the conquerer of Aetolia, to dedicate to him the altar over which Sant' Ambrogio is built. In Rome, Hercules was the giver of health as well as the giver of victory. The altar on which he had sacrificed at Rome was at the foot of the Aventine, and nearby was his temple containing the Ara Maxima. The Aetolians, however, claimed descent from Hercules and Nobilior's new temple. The nine confiscated Aetolian statues led, in fact, to Hercules becoming a second Apollo in Rome. Having brought back from Aetolia the nine statues of the muses, the Hercules of Nobilior's temple was known as Hercules Musagetes (Hercules the Muse-bearer).

Through his strength Hercules was the patron of many facets of life, both private and public. Though later officially demoted by a decree of Augustus, he never lost his popularity. After the fire of 80 c.e. (which damaged Titus' new and unfinished temple of Jupiter Capitolinus, as well as the Pantheon, the baths of Agrippa, the theatres of Pompey and Balbus, and the Porticoes of Philip and Octavia), one of the first monuments to be restored was the altar of Hercules under Sant' Ambrogio.

Hercules, however, was venerated not only as patron of the strong but as protector of the weak; victor and vanquished alike were his clients. This dual aspect ceases to be a paradox when we see that both sides were also reflected by Jesus: a comparison emphasized in the Middle Ages, when Hercules took his place with Virgil among the personages carved at the west door of so many cathedrals: Virgil, the pagan poet inspired to prophesy the coming of Christ; Hercules, the model for Christians who can enter the kingdom only after a life of hardship, struggle, and difficult tasks. Near the end of the thirteenth century, Hercules even replaced John the Baptist on the Seal of Florence, a substitution that surprises no one acquainted with the place given to Hercules in the writings of Justin Martyr, Cyril of Alexandria, Dom de Perseigne the Cistercian, and Dante. By the time of the Reformation both sides found it natural to call Jesus the Christian Hercules.

The Church has an obligation to be in touch with all who remain ignorant of Christ, an obligation fulfilled in all the centuries since the time of the apostles through the writings of medieval exegetes right down to the development of ecumenism in our own day. In connection with this, I am reminded of a recent message from the present bishop of Limoges urging people in his diocese not to limit themselves to Church activities but to be more aware that their duty as Christians is to those outside the Church.

Dom Simon Tonini has an interesting article in *AIM* for 1982 called "The Church, Non-Christians, and the Monk," in which he points out how strongly both Paul VI and John Paul II have urged us to be in touch with non-Christians. This, of course, is particularly clear to our monasteries in Asia, Africa, and Latin America. Their contacts, in fact, are kept up not only with non-Christians but with a growing number of Christians attracted to the spiritualities of Africa, Asia, and America. A parallel in Europe is the attraction to popular religious belief and devotional attitudes, since these are studies that are showing us how close we remain to our primitive human origins.

From what I have been saying, it seems to me that we can draw two conclusions:

a. First, *conversio* involves whatever is most primitive in ourselves, everything that has persisted through the millennia. This is implied by the saying that "God in the fullness of time has spoken to us through his son." We need always to be on guard against limiting our *conversio* to our more select layers—*conversio* has to affect everything in us that can be called human, however primitive or savage.

b. Second, whatever is noble in us comes from beliefs that, sincerely held, show themselves in the way we live and behave. Our faith cannot be studied in isolation from the many various religious beliefs we encounter; and the more we understand our own faith, the easier it is to avoid confusion and facile syncretism. This study of other beliefs must continue throughout our lives, for human *conversio* is nothing but the discovery of God revealing himself to us through our understanding of our own selves; and that means understanding all the most hidden of our latent paganisms. Life is what links human and divine. *Conversio* becomes impossible if we shut our eyes and ears to it; and this is so in Genesis and Deuteronomy, onward to the person of Christ, who is the incarnation of God's concern for us; and from this divine concern, our *conversio* is born when we listen to life.

2. Peter and Paul

A Benedictine, constantly reminded that *conversio* comes from attentive listening, should not be surprised that what we have been saying leads us to the topic of Peter and Paul, since the Word of God could never have been brought to us except by apostles who had listened attentively to it. It wasn't long ago that people found it natural to think of a Catholic Peter, a Protestant Paul, and an Orthodox Andrew, the sort of bogus simplification typical of all facile attempts to establish false oppositions and neat identities. Paul had to correct this tendency when dealing with the comparative value of pastors and doctors and all the other ministries in the Church; and James, when dealing with those who distinguished between Christians *with* and

Christians *without* a right to the first places. The same thing is only too familiar to us in our own monasteries; yet, fraternal conflicts don't have to be condemned as sterile, since some, at least, like the row between Peter and Paul, can be fruitful and end in an even closer harmony. A community is a place where the role of each member needs to be clarified in this sort of way before it can be lived to the benefit of all.

It would be tempting to pursue the subject, but here I am focusing on one aspect only: the need for *both* Peter *and* Paul, the need for the Word of God to be relayed by another if we are to hear it, and the need for us to relay it to others if they are to hear. Only when we come to see that the others are there, so that we are able to listen to them, can our *conversio* begin to include all the things inside us that make us human. It is this fact alone that makes the *conversio* of all the human race possible.

Yet, as well as being listened to, the Word also has to be accepted as a gift, which isn't quite the same as listening. Then it begins to affect the way we behave, and only then do we find that we are beginning to relay the Word of God to others. If we make Peter and Paul the patron apostles of proclaiming the Word of God in this way, then we can begin to understand the proper meaning of the word "witness" or "martyr." From these apostles we discover the meaning of "serving" God, of witnessing to truth until death. *Conversio* means being martyrs until we are martyred, living as life-long witnesses to life.

If, as I remember, the painting at Sant' Ambrogio shows the two apostles exchanging the kiss of peace and becoming reconciled, it may be worth thinking a bit about the quarrel they had. It grew out of two different ways Christians behave in the presence of non-Christians, ways we behave even in the presence of Christians who keep up the pieties, customs, and spirituality of their pre-Christian days. What is important is the need to understand how one's own behavior should proclaim to others that Christ the Savior came for the sake of all human beings. The iconography of the kiss of apostolic peace tells us that our search must be for an inner harmony between the different ways adopted by Peter and Paul to serve the Word as witnesses—martyrs—to truth.

The Church of Rome existed already before either Peter and Paul arrived on the scene, so neither can be called its founder. Rome claims to be *doubly* apostolic, the city of Peter and of Paul, the city of their union, of their harmony, of their peace. The monuments attesting to this double apostleship are well known and countless, even apart from all the misinterpreted or unhistorical details worked into this tradition of apostolic unanimity. We do not have to imagine that they were actually in Rome at the same time; that they met and appeared together before the imperial tribunal; that they were flogged simultaneously and in the same place as commemorated by the Church near Hadrian's Mausoleum; that they parted near the

Pyramid of Cestius, where the church of their separation now is; or that they died on the same day in the same year, jointly receiving from Christ the laurels of victory—as some imagine is commemorated in a certain catacomb referred to as *ad duas lauros*. Yet, behind all these cherished legends is the Roman awareness of being the apostolic city par excellence, receiving in Peter the reality of Christ's college of the Twelve, and accepting in Paul his claim to be, with them, equally, the apostle of Christ.

In these two apostles—Peter and Paul—are summed up the means that God chose for evangelizing the whole world, both Jewish and non-Jewish; the means chosen to bring about the *conversio* of all so that everything that is human might be incorporated into Christ through his Word that renews creation through being preached in unanimity by his apostles.

Dom Adalbert de Vogüé has pointed out how Pope Gregory's portrait of Benedict is intended to highlight his position in the line of transmission from prophet and apostle, exercising within his monastic community the power given Peter of binding and loosing, and through prayer receiving, like Paul, the safety of his companions threatened in a natural disaster. Here Dom Adalbert, himself, is in the line of all the early writers who describe the monastic and apostolic life in which poverty and humility eliminate concern for self while allowing the apostolic word to open the heart and mind. This even suggests how the wounded heart and open side are images not only of Christ but also of his disciples, since "heart" should always be taken in the sense of that wholeness which each of us is; the wholeness affected by *conversio,* the wholeness to be effected by our resurrection.

One might suggest that the president could have added the older mosaic icon of the Church shown twice in Rome at Saint Sabina: as a Jewish woman (*ecclesia ex circumcisione*) and as a Roman (*ecclesia ex gentibus*)—425 C.E.; and also the mosaic of Peter appointing two deputies: Linus and Cletus, one for Jewish Catholics and one for pagan converts.

3. Church and Synagogue

The gaping wound in the side of the Christian "body" is the absence of Israel, the Jewish Catholic Church. It is important to mention this here, since monasteries are intended by Benedict to be places with a special ability to reflect upon this wound, places where we can never avoid being aware of the separation of synagogue and church, never forget the Jewishness of Jesus, which alone makes sense of the economy of salvation; never forget what he is and what he did, for this alone can identify our own monastic *conversio* as Christians. Père Bouyer once pointed out that the divisions within the Church, whether between East and West or Protestant and Catholic, are no more than historical facts that have affected the health of the Church but which could be easily cured; whereas the disease from which the Bride of the Lamb is suffering is one that makes it unworthy of the banquet, for it is we who have failed with regard to the Jews, beginning with that total indifference to the Church of the Jewish Catholics as it was being whittled away to nothing. This is a disease that threatens not only the health but the very life of the Church, for it deprives Christian history of any meaning. Apostolic *conversio* imposes on us a particular obligation to help in removing these shackles; but also, like every Christian who wants to enter more deeply into the mystery, we have to relive in our spiritual development the entire history of the Jewish people. This is a journey imposed on all monks by their *conversio,* a pilgrimage totally incompatible with the myth that Jewish Catholicism was a temporary phenomenon destined by Jesus to disappear with the triumph of the *ecclesia ex gentibus.*

We have spoken in previous letters of the "sign of contradiction." We see it here again in the synagogue, which manifests it to anyone not Jewish by birth or religion, and reminds us that Christianity is intended for all peoples, nations, and cultures, for all the periods of history throughout the whole of time. To realize the full meaning of the word "contradiction" as used in Scripture, we have to think deeply about it. We can say that in Christ the divine and creating Word "contradicts" the human nature it created; but that doesn't mean it destroys it or disowns it but rather raises it to a greater and previously unheard of reality: it divinizes the human. In the section of this letter where I discuss *fuga mundi,* we shall be able to look far more closely at this word *contradictio.* At the moment I want to point out merely that it is an indication of the double task we have as human beings; witnessing to the one vocation of all human beings in the whole of human history, in every part of the world; and witnessing to how we receive from Christ a new relationship to the rest of the cosmos, the entire universe of created reality. No Christian *conversio,* no monastic *conversio,* could exist without this cosmic dimension.

Human history has known many ways of expressing religion, of being religious; but the religion of the people of God was the one ready for the Word—himself the sign of contradiction—who came to fulfill what had already evolved to the point where it was ready for that fulfillment, ready to become the seed of a universal religious pattern. When I say that what Christ brought is universal, I do not mean that it has anything to do with uniformity. Monastic *conversio* is universal, but there is nothing uniform about the life of monasteries in Africa, Asia, America, and Europe, though each remains a sign of that specifically Christian contradiction which is death *and* resurrection.

Please remember that everything in this part of the letter—everything to do with Hercules and his altar, with the synagogue and Rome, with the synagogue and Scripture, with Peter and Paul as models of all *conversio,* with their kiss of peace as sign of harmony between the Church *ex circumcisione* and the Church *ex gentibus*—all this and the rest that I have mentioned is an epiphany taking place (as Scripture is so vividly aware) in the real cosmos. All this is meant as an introduction to the more pentecostal theme of our *fuga mundi*.

I offer this introduction because it represents my reactions to the many indigenous cultures I have met while traveling around the world, and since I travel for your sake, it has seemed right to share them with you. Among these cultures I have met the Diaspora of Israel, and it is this which has forced me to rethink the meaning of Paul and the synagogue, the meaning of the sign of contradiction, the meaning of Jesus "the only friend of all our human race" (a phrase from the Greek liturgy), the "just one among all the nations," the beloved of the most high (blessed be he) whose death outside the walls of Jerusalem made of Golgotha the new center of a world waiting and ready for its *conversio* to the God of Abraham, Isaac, and Jacob. That said, we can now turn to the *fuga mundi*.

It is absurd, however, and perhaps even a little silly to try to express in a few pages all that is meant by *fuga mundi* or "flight from the world." Because all of you who have made the decision to become and remain Benedictine nuns and monks and have already devoted much thought to this topic, there won't be any need to try to cover *all* that is meant by the phrase. What I shall offer will simply be suggestions that might (or might not) help you to clarify your ideas, to understand the direction that your flight—your journey through life—has been gradually taking. By now, even the novices will be aware that this flight, whatever else it is meant to be away from, is never going to be away from the risks and temptations of life. However, though I don't have to cover *all* aspects of *fuga mundi*, I still have to fit what I want to say into a few pages. I only hope you will not think my remarks superficial. As usual, I shall divide the topic into three:

1) What on earth do we mean by this "world" from which we flee?
2) What do people mean who have begun to say it is better to think of "the world" as fleeing from *us*?
3) What is the true Benedictine flight when considered as part of the new vista opened up by Christ?

Part II: Pentecost 1983

1. What Is this World from Which Monks Flee?

To understand this we must remember the pagan as well as the Jewish concepts of "flight." On the one hand, there have been attempts at "flight" from everything material and intelligible, flight from a world thought to be infested with demons and evil forces, flight from the hardships and trials of everyday life, flight—especially nowadays by the underprivileged—from the world of illiteracy, starvation, and all the social conditions that encourage deprivation. These are all flights inspired by fear; but there are, on the other hand, flights inspired by love. If we turn to Benedict, we find that he speaks of flight toward everlasting life and away from *Gehenna,* flight toward the perpetual remembrance of God, flight toward what God has promised to those who love him; but nowhere in the Rule is there any mention of monks fleeing "from the world," or any hint of monks "despising the world." On the contrary, the cellarer is told to be as careful about the "things of this world" as he is about the "things of God." Benedict says nothing at all about the world being infested with cosmic demons. On the contrary, he reflects a clear understanding that our *conversio,* our search for God and our encounter with God, takes place *in* the world, that monks belong to the world and specifically to the world of human freedom. We see his attitude implied in the way he uses the concept of Jacob's Ladder, and we see it in his concept of our hearts being opened.

Jacob's Ladder, in Genesis, proves to Jacob that God is close, that God is with him; so much so that when Jacob wakes he can say that this is the place where God *is.* This is also Benedict's meaning of the Ladder, and to it he adds that the living Ladder, composed of angels, is nothing more than what we do *in* this world. The angelic Ladder is composed of our human deeds, the deeds of our body and mind carried out in this place where we encounter God and are united to him. It is a place of freedom, as Benedict shows in the passage on the opening of the heart that we experience after entering the narrow gate and begin our journey along the road we travel in liberty with swiftness and spiritual joy.

Benedict never confuses flight *from the world* with flight *to God:* it is that *to* which we are fleeing, and that only, which makes us monks. Far from leaving the world, it is *in* this world that good zeal becomes the fruit of eternal life, which is the capacity to love all others without exception or preference, beginning with our confrères whom we meet in daily life. Our freedom of heart is the freedom of God living through us. Is it a paradox that the Rule tells us both to run and to remain stable? Not really, because the cenobitic life is what establishes the condition for our progress through love, that is, our union with others, the center of balance or gravity that is needed for sustained flight. On those days when our mental weather clears and we can see spiritual things with unusual sharpness, we can actually detect how it is that stability and the burdens of love increase the speed of our flight.

What is much more of a paradox is to find that the first result of cenobites fleeing to God is for them to be established even more firmly as part of the world's social, public, and economic life. As cenobites our daily progress toward the fullness of life is made up of prayer, office, work, and hospitality, all of them immediate links in time and space between the monk and others. This is especially true of work and hospitality, both of which are essentials in monastic life. Indeed, for the Benedictine, the Rule makes work and hospitality the indicators of whether a monastery is the house of God, since the monk—like God, like Christ—must work and must welcome every stranger.

Being human, we cannot expect work and hospitality to always be carried out perfectly in monasteries. We actually must expect the occasions when we bungle, when our flight toward God is off course, frequently so much off course that we find we are flying away from God and toward ourselves. How easy, for instance with guests, to find ourselves being selective, excluding types we don't find congenial and preferring those we do. Yet, since the time of Benedict, the Benedictine ideal of hospitality to all without exception and with equal honor is the ideal that has perhaps been adhered to most faithfully through the centuries. We receive every guest in the spirit of pure humanity. One hears of monasteries that observe this to the letter and yet always manage to keep their guests at arm's length—if monks are capable of lacking in generosity, guests are capable of lacking in discretion. Insofar as this is the case, then neither can claim to be one of "the Poor." They are simply playing the standard game of pretense and half-truth, which denies the Benedictine tradition of hospitality, especially as it was practiced during difficult periods of history and in dangerous places. As far as work is concerned, Benedict must smile at the kinds of attempts we make to correct the direction of our flight, particularly when it is a question of work that happens to be essential, or that we think is suitably "monastic," or that we believe we can carry out according to professional standards, or that the whole community can be proud of. Still, who knows whether these little temporal satisfactions are not something we need in order to experience the way we are going to appreciate our future transition into real and everlasting glory?

So far we have spoken about "the world" in a rather traditional way; but nowadays the word implies something larger and we need a broader vision. "World" is a word that has turned out to be more enigmatic and ambiguous than it used to seem. For one thing, both the earth and the cosmos have turned out to be considerably larger; they are also turning out to be less definable as well as far more subtly present in our subconscious. Whereas Scripture is concerned with the nature of the human being, we have to face the problem of what life is, of how matter and spirit are connected.

2. Is the World Itself Fleeing from Monks?

From our own experience of the flight to God, we learn the need to be constantly adjusting and readjusting our intentions in order to avoid the sort of pitfalls we mentioned when talking about work and hospitality, about the ways in which we are present in the world and to the world. Prayer is the ideal time for making these readjustments and reorienting ourselves, and we are all aware that we never make nearly as much as we should of the opportunities for prayer that come our way. We are quite aware that this is the chief way in which we fail to make progress in our flight to God, aware how frequently we are in the condition of forgetting to see ourselves and observe the way we relate to God. This condition of forgetfulness is, in fact, what constitutes "the world" *from* which we flee.

The three most obvious ways in which we relate to others are:

a. When by "others" we mean all who have not renounced marriage, possessions, and the freedom to dispose of their time and energies;
b. When by "others" we mean the rest of the Church that has not chosen to enter the monastic state;
c. When we mean not just "others" but "the Other," that is, God.

How, then, do we relate to these three: world, Church, and God? How do they relate to each other? Benedict, for instance, relates them both in his vision of the whole cosmos as no larger than a speck of dust, and in his image of Jacob's Ladder. In each case he is indicating how the goal is our union with God and how short the road is that leads to that goal. In each case, too, he is indicating how, in the things of God, the farthest is the nearest and the greatest is the least.

We need also, of course, to keep in mind the work of all the great theologians and philosophers who have examined these relationships of God, world, and Church, and have examined the meaning of the word "relationship." We need to reflect on what we mean by the word and by the three realities: to reflect on God as both liberator and creator; on the world and its human inhabitants and the unlimited possibilities they present; on the Church as founded by God to lead the human to the divine. When I say we need to reflect on these and remember them, it is because it is so important for us not to misunderstand this catch phrase of "flight from the world," important because it is so often misunderstood and so fatally easy to misunderstand. Things probably seemed neater when people thought of the earth as the center of a tiny cosmos hardly larger than our planetary system, when they thought of the Church as having incorporated virtually the whole human race. If the monastery was a model of the cosmos, the whole of the universe was a cosmic monastery. The Christian realism of today that reacts against these older and neater views could nevertheless learn a great deal from what Père de Lubac has written about Abbot Joachim of Flora and his spiritual posterity.

As monks we have to grow accustomed to the idea that we live at one and the same time both at the heart and center of the Church and on its outermost frontiers. Though part of the human race that has a single goal, monks have assumed a special obligation of aiming at that goal which lies in the direction so clearly seen by Benedict and the Rule, a direction that was opened by Christ at Easter in order to help the totality of the human race to accelerate its flight along that path or freeway to the light which von Balthasar calls the "Paschal Vista."

3. The Paschal Vista Opened by Christ

The genius, and so the greatness, of Benedict lies in the way he was able to center the whole of monastic life, even as an organized structure, on the single mystery of Easter and Pentecost, on what is revealed by this vista unblocked and opened by Christ and the Holy Spirit. The history of every monastic community reflects this event even during those periods when its progress has been slowed down and its path has led through the desert—provided, of course (since these things don't happen automatically), that the community remain conscious of the focus a monastic community has.

People often wonder what, if anything, there is that can be called *new* in what Jesus taught. His sayings about God being love, about loving one's enemies, about not judging others, only affirm what has long been accepted as sound Jewish orthodox theology. Jesus was far from being the first Jew to perform miracles, and not even the first to emphasize the virtue of hope. His uniqueness lay not in what he taught but in what he was, in his relationship to the Father. Indeed, the whole of Israel is the Son of God and all the Israelites are his children. Jesus, however, was uniquely the Son of the Father, and from the outset he was acknowledged as such in Bethlehem and again when he was twelve, and also when he lived at Nazareth and when in Jerusalem. We could mention, too, the newness not of his life but of his death and its proclamation of the mystery of the Nothing and the All, since the essence of this paschal vista, this culmination of the life, death, and resurrection of Jesus, is how the Nothing proclaims the All, revealing Jesus as truly the Son.

With the unblocking of our view, with the breakthrough and opening of the vista, we see more clearly the direction in which we are to fly, the direction called in Scripture the Future or the Days to Come. Abraham owned nothing of the promised land except the plot in which he was eventually buried; Moses gained nothing of it but his view from Pisgah, and even after the entry, the conquered pagans were able to tempt the faith of the victors. In that land, however, God's people, having glimpsed the glory that was to come in the future and from above, could begin the search, the forward flight, always anticipating that God would fulfill his promise, always aware that the path of faith is endless, always conscious that the Promised One would enlighten all nations, peoples, and places. As Christians, we see this fulfillment come about when Jesus—the only truly living one who said "I am the life"—removed the obstacle which is death, and revealed the resurrection.

This is our faith and there is nothing in it to make us "strangers to the human race" and aliens to the rest of humanity—unless we imagine that the divine promise is now exhausted and that nothing remains to be given. Yet, it is possible that this faith can explain why those who think they have rejected it or who think they could never accept it can feel themselves at a distance from us, and can imagine that this is so because we are "fleeing" from them. If our flight forward were what they imagine it to be, a flight away from others, we would not be part of the global flight of humanity forward to our destiny. For those who cannot hear of this forward progress in our theological terminology toward the One—toward union with God—it has to be expressed in terms even more mysterious, obscure, and ambiguous than our own.

Not long ago writers in France were making much of our present human crisis. They called it "the death of Man," what Merleau-Ponty called "this absence of the Inner." There was a definition, much debated, of the human as "pure liberty," as existing truly only in the "free Act"; yet this was found to deny any possibility of a bridge from one human to another, not to mention cutting off every chance of a bridge to the Other. I mention this as an example of how a monastery is always situated firmly in the culture of its own time, and of how our own contemporary culture has led us quite recently to a reassessment of the *fuga mundi* theme by providing a closer and more attentive observation of our own innerness.

4. Conclusion

Fuga Mundi is:
   a. a personal choice made at our own innermost center;
   b. a way of actually loving, a way so valuable that, while it prevents a human from remaining stationary, it allows us to make progress only by the progressive discovery of all the implications and complications it entails; this is what Benedictine discernment is, distinguishing more and more clearly between the things that prevent our development and the things that encourage it;
   c. a personal gift to each of us, intended to enhance and increase the value we place on others as human persons, and in particular a gift that enables us to do this through appreciating our own self as person; a gift that Benedict calls "obedience" (*ob-audientia*), a gift of *listening,* a gift that creates bridges between people;

    d. a process that involves *choice*, meaning that we can speak (poetically) of the "death" of all the possible things that we decide against or (to vary the metaphor) we can speak of our death to them;

    e. it is the progressive lessening of our selfish grasp of the life; and by loosening this grasp, by eliminating what is selfish about it, we become free to make progress toward what life is;

    f. our growth in the ability to *love* the world, the elimination of any hatred or despising of the world, the world of human beings, of human values; and in doing this we have the obligation of listening to them, of perceiving their needs and wants and requirements;

    g. it is flight away from what is selfish (i.e., sinful), away from the self-love that prevents our love of others (cf. Evagrius on *apatheia* as loving others without exception or preference).

Jesus said "follow me." Our *fuga mundi* is our lifelong flight toward the Father to whom Jesus leads us (cf. Père Carmignac on the Lord's Prayer: lead us "not into," i.e., "lead us out of" temptation, to the Father). *Fuga mundi* has no room for any of that "hatred of the human race" of which Roman pagans accused converts to Israel and to Christianity. There is no room for that "angelism" which involves a flight from what the Manichees and Gnostics considered the evil of matter and of bodies. Flight away from other humans, away from anything God created, is the opposite of what Benedict teaches us.

Our Benedictine following of Jesus to the Father is, however, most certainly "spiritual," since it is brought about by the Holy Spirit Jesus sent us from the Father, the same Holy Spirit that gradually purifies and constantly reorients the direction of our flight and ensures that it is humanist and Christian, intimately concerning us with all others (whether visibly in the Church or not) who are also searching for the meaning of life. There remains, of course, the one aspect of "the world" from which we *are* in flight, and this is the selfish self-centeredness which alone can block the Easter vista opened by Christ to reveal the mystery in which, through the Holy Spirit, we participate by the monastic flight to God.

Denis Huerre, *Abbot-president*
Congregation of Subiaco
Sant' Ambrogio, Rome

On Stability

To All the Members of Our Congregation:

The superior of one of our monasteries suggested that I devote this letter to the topic of *stability,* and I do so willingly; for all superiors, like her, not only need to help their subjects but must do so in circumstances that make it impossible to escape the distractions of a busy life. Stability, of course, is one of the means offered to all who aim at true *conversio,* and so the topic fits in very neatly with the previous letters of this series. Those who have already made their profession will have devoted a great deal of thought to stability—yet not one of us has succeeded in becoming what we should be. As usual I shall divide the letter into three points: 1) Benedict and stability; 2) attaining stability by degrees; 3) God living his own stability in us.

1. Benedict on Stability

Having read through the Rule a great many times, I would describe it as intended for those who *truly* seek to share the *true* life of the *true* God. By underlining the word "true," I want to emphasize one of Benedict's preoccupations, which is his awareness of the dangers of illusion, of taking false turns. We can notice this in his concern for our fidelity to the true faith, to our faith in the Holy Trinity.

At the level of human spirituality, Stability and Truth are almost interchangeable terms in the Rule because instability robs us of our security and freedom and makes us less than human. To turn away from faith in the Trinity, as so many were tempted to do in the sixth century—away, that is, from professing faith in the divinity of Christ our Savior—is to deny that Christ can be our Savior. He is Savior because he is true man and true God; if he were only someone pointing the way to God, a monastery could no longer have its raison d'être in the paschal mystery. The salvation of the world depends on the relationship of our human nature to the Trinity; but given that this is just as clear to us as it was to Benedict, let us turn to consider the *site,* the *bond,* and the *aim* as three elements of monastic stability;

and then go on to see how Benedict brings them all together into one image of the house founded on rock.

a. Stability and Site

We make our profession in relation to a specific monastery, and all the other later monastic groupings (congregation, federation, union, etc.) are intended only to strengthen this basic concept; and this they do by assisting a monastery when it is going through a difficult time. In particular they make it possible for that monastery to safeguard its autonomy, that is, its ability to form its own members by offering them stability. It is because of this stability that monks can really care for their monastery, for the setting in which they live their life. It is why Benedictines can have a truly human concern for their house, why they can take an intelligent and affectionate interest in it—and all the more so when they do this, knowing that it is only a temporary shelter afforded us while on the way to our true home above.

Stability helps us appreciate this paradox of our incessant traveling between the visible and the invisible, the paradox of our perpetual incarnation and our perpetual spiritualization. The site has almost always been chosen because it has seemed suitable for the setting in which we make our pilgrimage to God. As our stability fosters such a perspective, it becomes a habit for us to see the monastery as our true home, even though it is one where we spend a lifetime looking forward to an eternal home. Deprived of this aim, this ultimate goal, the monastery would swallow us and probably turn into our prison.

The monastery is the place where we live our lives, yet we do not live *for* it; we live for the sake of God and for the sake of all our fellow creatures. This is the more important aspect of our life in the monastery, and it leads us to consider the problem of those who feel they must therefore leave in order either to live a life in closer union with God or a life of greater service to other people. It is a problem to which we shall return; but when discussing it, we will have to remember that we should never underrate the importance of a community having a strong human psychological relationship with the place in which it lives. This is the earthly side of what we mean when talking of the union of heaven and earth. It means that it will always be more normal for the monk to remain attached to his monastic home than for him to move away. To feel the need for change can be a sign of something other than seeking God.

b. Stability and Bond

It is obvious that the rule intends our stability to be a free choice but it may not be quite so obvious that Benedict realized how stability can be

the means of achieving our freedom. It is because we are human that Christ
is concerned with our inner freedom; and it can never be simply because
we are monks or Christians that stability and freedom are so closely inter-
related. The bond created by our stability is an aspect of that covenant into
which we enter with Christ; that, indeed, is why we choose to make our
profession during the offertory. We nearly always speak of having made "our
own" profession, when, in fact, it is not made only by ourselves: it is made
between ourselves and the whole community. The community and the
newly professed make a joint renewal of the covenant with God, and dispensation from vows will always be a concern of the community and not
just of one solitary member. As solemn undertakings made in public, our
vows are the concern of all Christians and even of the public at large, which
can be quite genuinely shocked when a dispensation is granted. They see
it as the Church granting monks the equivalent of a divorce which she refuses to married couples. It even destroys all credibility in the Mass, that
covenant sealed in the Body and Blood of Christ, which we choose as the
public setting for our vows.

When any professed members of the community remain faithful to their
profession, it is the entire community that is being faithful, and the whole
community rejoices. This is why we must always remember the possibility
that when a member leaves a community, it is those who remain behind,
faithful to their vows, who may deserve the greater blame. Monasteries must
always be alert lest we be found wanting in the mutual love implied by every
monastic profession, which is the bond that gives us the stability that makes
our freedom possible.

c. Stability and Aim

Stability is not something that freezes us into immobility. It offers us
the possibility of living as humans, that is, living with an aim, with a goal.
I am still hoping to devote a future letter to the role in our life of the aim,
the goal—desire and love. I include it here because this alone is what justi-
fies the stability we profess. With stability, Benedict offers us a joy that cannot
be separated from the solidarity of the community. He offers us something
meant to enhance our life, something that is Eucharistic because it is related to that union established by Holy Communion, just as our choice
for the setting of our monastic life is not made because the site is desirable,
but because we find God to be desirable. If the tools of good works include
concupiscence for God, it is because our aim is not to eliminate but to spiritu-
alize what is human. God is still acting as our Creator when his spirit trans-
forms all those tensions that go to make up a human life. Looking this way
at our goal and aim, we can see how *place, vows, and love* are three strands
that go to make up our stability. Benedict makes use of an image that helps
us see even more clearly the place that our stability has in the mystery of

Christ. Scripture draws from a wide range of images to speak of the Creator's work among his creation. Benedict has selected just one of these, that of the house founded on rock.

d. *The Stability of a House Founded on Rock*

Among the scriptural images that we can find helpful to our meditation on the mystery of salvation—the laborer, the harvest, the winepress, the banquet, the daily bread, the wedding feast, the journey, the spiritual weapons, the mystical body, etc., Benedict has found one to which he reverts constantly: the image of our life with God as his household, a household that he has founded on rock. Repeatedly spoken of by psalmists and prophets and New Testament writers, it has provided Christ with many of his titles, such as cornerstone, foundation, door, light, etc. Now floodwaters may threaten to sweep away the house founded on sand, but water itself is essential if we are to live in a house; and Christ is that water. We could never make use of a house if we could not get in through the door; and Christ is the door. These are the sort of images that come together when Benedict is suggesting that stability is an ideal means for us to choose if we are truly seeking God. The rock that ensures stability to the house is the Word of God, which is Christ himself. Not the word as simply heard, read, studied, or meditated upon, but the word of life actually listened to and actually performed in our life. The waters that threaten—whether by sudden torrent or by a slowly rising flood level—to sweep away the house, come into the Rule from the psalms, where they symbolize the need for that spiritual warfare which constitutes the monastic art—not so much an art of swimming as the art of simply withstanding assault. That art we learn from Job (35), how the Word of God sufficed to hold back the waters and keep them at a respectful distance.

It is possible that we may not have noticed that Christ, as the door, has his place in the Rule, when Benedict speaks of the porter, when he teaches us the spiritual art of monastic hospitality as training us for the great day of the apocalypse, when the doors of our heavenly home will stand wide open forever. Indeed, this reminds me that at some time I must write about the harmony between *conversio* and hospitality. Here I shall simply point out that we must apply this Benedictine art of the porter in an extended sense that includes mail, telephone, and radio. It is the door in this extended sense that brings us face to face with the meaning of stability.

If it's quite natural for monks to have a genuine affection for their monastery, it is because their delight is in the fact that the life they pass in a particular topographical setting is spent in passing from Christ to Christ, from Alpha to Omega. Stability certainly isn't meant to imply that life spent in this way will be uneventful—we all know how easily it develops into a drama.

2. Achieving Stability by Degrees

Stability is as long as the rest of our life; it is part of our autobiography, which is to say, it is part of the history of our development, a development which is generally gradual and which we can think of as having three main stages:

a. Stage 1

After postulancy and novitiate, after initial hesitations and much thought, the first stage begins when we reach that decision which in most cases brings its own deep sense of inner stability. No one can say if young people in 1984 find it easier or harder than young people of 1950, 1000, or 500, but on the whole it would seem probably true that having made that decision, they will have far more excuses than people did in the past to reconsider it. This is true even though the decision was reached as it always has been reached after a period of intense anguish. Once the decision has been made, it is nearly always accompanied by a feeling of fulfillment, an awareness that remains vivid enough to be a real help when we encounter the inevitable periods of crisis later on. We can even be surprised at how much strength we get from the recollection of that moment of decision, especially when we go through the worst moments of being totally unsettled; and yet this strength is understandable, since that moment of decision really is a unique and privileged moment in our life, the one moment we were sufficiently free to assert our freedom.

b. Stage 2

The second stage of stability naturally begins the moment something threatens to undermine it, and the things that do this range all the way from feeling a need to gossip to feelings of violent claustrophobia or some other effect of psychological strain. In between the two extremes come all those varying degrees of distraction marked by the urge to do something, to create something; this is often marked by periods of intense activity, of absolute boredom, of total disenchantment, or simply finding one's self a bit envious. Usually, of course, we are reacting to something, and often it does not matter in the least what it is we are reacting to—whether it is the government, the Church, or a neighbor in the community. However trivial or serious the thing may be against which we react, the one important thing is what our reaction is revealing to ourselves about ourselves. Revelations like these can be dangerous and are usually painful and often brutal; yet they are normal and, in spite of any threat they pose to our stability, they are healthy. The only real danger is when they are naively taken as something diabolical when, in fact, they are simply the way God speaks to monks and asks us questions. Having created us with the ability to think and reflect and understand, it is probably the only way he can ask us questions, the only way he can get us to change direction and set a new course.

This second stage of stability is the one in which we progressively discover our limitations, that is to say, in which we discover the truth about ourselves, a truth that usually turns out to be not quite as simple as we expected. Above all—and most importantly—it is the stage when we are forced to discover what it means to be a creature, to discover our nothingness, and so to discover the divine through discovering what we are not; the stage when God prompts us to rethink our ideas about ourself and about the rest of the world, to readjust all of our previous convictions, and to reaffirm our stability by locating its foundations at levels we hadn't previously expected. We are not meant to find these reassessments attractive. These are not the changes that appeal to us, and yet they are essential if we are to live our lives naturally and authentically in harmony with our innermost truth and with the truth that is Christ. Every monastery is aware of how upsetting this second stage can be, even provoking storms in the whole community. We must never let ourselves be surprised when these happen. The only question is whether we should welcome them or resent them as a nuisance—and that is a question to which we ought to devote some serious thinking. Of one thing we can be sure: many members of our communities would never have left the monastery if the fraternal help they had a right to expect had been more forthcoming.

c. *Stage 3*

These upsets and disturbances do not last forever. Our road widens on the other side of Benedict's narrow door. Stability, however, is something that takes place on two levels: one is in the heart, where the decision is not only made but desired; the other is at the level of our activities, where it is still a matter of will rather than of passions and surface reactions. Each time we reenter the realm of the heart to hear the Word of God, each time we listen to what the divine presence has to say, we encounter our true and inner stability, we find that our feet are firmly set on the road after all.

Every monastery is aware of some members who quite obviously have this true stability in God. They simply jump over all the obstacles and can always be counted upon to show real compassion for anyone who seems to be wobbling. They seem to get along with people as easily as they get along with God, and they are always marked by a total lack of fanaticism. For most of us, stability is something that grows, that seems to become stronger as we grow older and wiser; yet we do meet those others who reach stability precociously, who seem to inherit some atavistic ability of coping with anything. Nothing upsets them, nothing troubles their stability; and above all, they have the supreme gift of compassion—they never adopt a holier-than-thou attitude, and never give the impression of wanting to keep their distance. They are the ones who help the rest of us keep our balance, who go a long way toward helping us keep our stability. (At the other end of the spectrum are the grumblers, with nothing constructive to offer.) What we must all come to realize is that the stability we aim at isn't going to be reached by gritting our teeth, and still less by hanging on through sheer willpower. The stability we aim for is something we reach by charity, by being helpful to each other—the stability of a true community life.

3. Our Stability as Lived by God

There was a time when monasteries pretended to be fortresses and tried to imitate the stability of Jerusalem, the impregnable city. More recently we have seen barricades coming down and monasteries going to the other extreme and becoming models of openness. Both extremes produced more problems than solutions, but, unfortunately, the simple fact is that there is not any ideal architectural design for a monastery; so let us turn instead to its ideal architect.

The architect of creation is also the architect of the temple and both creation and the temple are *the* house of God par excellence. Behind this lies the deeper perspective taken up in the New Testament that sees the human race and each member of it as the dwelling place of God. Once, when von Balthasar was addressing the Benedictine and Cistercian abbots, he pointed out the parallels between John the Evangelist and Benedict in a commentary on a passage in the Gospel where we are told the Father and the Son take up their abode in the heart of those who hear and do the Word of God. The verb *menō* (*meneo:* to *remain,* tarry, abide) gives us both "monastery" and "monk"; yet the monastery becomes the house of God and a sign of his presence only when God is actually in residence, when both Word and Spirit are present (as Congar has said), revealing the Father to us (as Rahner has put it), since it is by speaking to us that God reveals his presence in us.

None of this should be taken, of course, to mean that some monasteries are not better off when they are better designed, but the inhabitants are more important than the building, and the important thing is that they should be waiting for God, waiting for him to speak and reveal himself; even though they are certain that when he does so, what he says will be relevant to the present, and usually disturbing. It is in this attitude of the inhabitants that we will find the true stability of the monastery and its community. We must be prepared to understand that the stability of monks consists in our readiness to have our routine disturbed, our readiness to find how it is through these disturbances that God opens his conversation, our readiness to discover that God brings about our *conversio* by dragging us into moments of total nothingness, moments that, in retrospect, are seen as our truest periods of spiritual happiness. We also discover how this is different from the nothingness of oblivion, the nothingness of the Stoics, the nothingness of recent philosophers; since it is the nothingness at our center that reveals God to be ceaselessly present and to be present as our Savior.

We have moved on a bit from the topic of stability to the coming of God because it is his advent that creates our stability. To see this and to live in its realization is to see the whole universe, beginning with our own monastery, in a new light; to see things everywhere as having acquired a new value, so that now no matter what happens at any time, every single thing that exists becomes the place of our encounter with God—and in this we discover our stability.

I have gone on too long already and still I haven't said all that I wanted to say, whether to those who have newly taken up the weapons of the Spirit in our battle for stability or to those who are struggling to preserve their stability with no one (perhaps even suspecting the fact) or, finally, to those who have experienced the joy of coming to realize that only God is stable and that we can speak about our stability only insofar as he shares his stability with us.

May all of you come to share that supreme stability in Christ which is our passage into love out of fear, out of that fear which is all too often the human aspect of a monastic life, a life that is truly monastic only when we can live it without fear of any one in the community, whether superiors or others; but above all without fear of God, who alone can realize our need and desire to live in his love. Whatever happens, never live in fear of life, because it is this life, here on earth, that constitutes God's epiphany to us, revealing himself, as the light by which every human nation and race makes progress toward the fullness of light. As monks we advance along that same road, not a separate one; and stability in our chosen place, through the vows we have chosen to make, is what allows us to hope that God himself will fulfill our desire for God.

Denis Huerre, *Abbot-president*
Congregation of Subiaco
Sant' Ambrogio, Rome

Pentecost 1984

"Conversio" and Guests

Dear Brothers and Sisters,

Two of your letters have been about guests: one suggesting that the decision made in the writer's community "has probably been beneficial to the groups that stay with us, but quite certainly not beneficial to the spiritual life of the community itself"; the other suggesting that our constitutions (which require the votes of the council or community in certain cases) were obviously aimed at reducing the number of long-stay guests; it even goes on to wonder if the Rule intended the reception of guests to be as essential in our life as work, prayer, and *lectio*. The writer thinks it possible that though Benedict may have intended that it would be normal for us to welcome any guests that arrive, he may have supposed that the arrival of the guests themselves would be something exceptional—and if this were not the case, might we not have monks saying they became Benedictines in order to practice hospitality?

Let me mention an occasion when I consulted Paul VI about something connected with my monastery: he told me "But the Holy See was never intended for solving those problems, that is why you have a Rule." I asked him at least to make a suggestion and he said: "Tell them to be frequent in prayer and attentive to guests, especially priest guests." If we agree that each monastery has to make its own decision on how to receive guests and even decide why they should be received, let us do so in the awareness that more and more people are expecting us to offer them a welcome and that bishops in every continent are asking us to provide it.

As Benedictines we should know both what a monk ought to be and yet how to fulfill what others expect of us. This is particularly obvious in the matter of guests, since though it isn't the most sublime aspect of our vocation, it is the most characteristic. In this letter we shall see if there is any light that can be shed on the question.

1. The Christian Understanding of Our Monastery as the House of God

Benedict often conveys a contemplative flavor in the way he speaks about something, and this is the case when he calls a monastery the "house of

God," the first implication of which is that we ourselves are the guests in the monastery, and God is our host. So fundamental is this that Benedict makes it the basis of our day-to-day poverty and, consequently, any idea we have of what our own monastery ought to be must begin with this fact, which becomes so obvious when we think of guests knocking at our door; it isn't our door at all they are knocking on but the same door at which we too have knocked, asking God, like them, to be guests in his house.

If a monastery is the house of God, then it isn't just the place where God is, but the place where he manifests his presence, his glory; and more than that, the house actually is God who is offering his welcome, "and this is a marvel in our sight" because this marvel of God's presence can't depend in any way on us or on our prayer or on our acts of courtesy, for these things are produced by his presence, which moves us to spontaneous blessing and doxology every time we become aware of it, as in the moment of a guest's arrival, for that is always an epiphany of God, a real presence of Christ.

"Blessing and doxology" are two of the most important words in Scripture, and Benedict uses them both in the chapter on guests. Every epiphany has two aspects: not only is God manifest, but where he is manifest there is the new humanity, the people that he is gathering together. It is as God's guests that we can assemble as monks for the sake of the guest who is arriving. There is a great depth in this vision that sees Christ himself equally present in both monks and guests. Christ opens the door to a stranger and it is Christ who knocks at that door. Christ as host receives Christ as guest, and Christ as guest recognizes Christ as host: monk and guest alike are Christ in his Father's house.

In the Rule, we are given two liturgies of welcome: one for the postulant seeking to be a long-staying guest, and one for the visitor asking to be a temporary guest. In each of them it is Christ's arrival that is celebrated, a new moment in the assembling of that people God is gathering into the new humanity. To avoid all misunderstanding, Benedict emphasizes this by allowing no distinction of person: all human beings are to be equally welcome since, in each, the mystery of salvation is being accomplished.

The obligation of hospitality is so grave that no form of monasticism is without it. Once, when I had responsibility for a brother hermit, I was surprised at first when he said how much he wished he were not so restricted by the enclosure of the monastery. Hermits are not recluses, and yet even recluses have always welcomed those who went to them. Hermits, then, should also be able to fulfill this command; and thus it is that semi-hermits as well as cenobites in charterhouses are able to welcome guests, as I discovered on one occasion for which I shall always be grateful.

There is simply no way that I can see in which we can avoid the fact that the reception of guests is absolutely essential to a monastery. One of the two letter writers said he had read a book on the Rule (by an author that I also admire) that didn't even have a chapter on guests; but such a chapter could deal with little more than the techniques of making guests feel welcome, since a monk is essentially one who welcomes all and everyone; he welcomes the Word of God, his brethren, the difficulties of life; and eventually he welcomes death. To all these he is able to offer a welcome because in each he sees the face of God. But for this grace to have a single welcome for all beings means that we have to reflect not just on the monastery as the house of God but also on the freedom that alone makes it possible for us to carry out the gospel: the freedom to welcome and to be welcomed.

2. The Liberty of Monk and Guest

God, Scripture, and the Rule all require us to welcome others, and this is a commandment we must always be ready to obey promptly: we have "to *hasten* to welcome the guest." Fr. Borias, who has written about the differences between the two liturgies of welcome, has shown how the second modifies the first and how neither is quite as simple as it seems. To understand them we have to go back to what is meant by "obeying God." To obey (as in Hebrew) is both to *listen* and to *do* something about it.

Starting with Genesis, this double aspect of obedience turns up in every part of Scripture. In monastic obedience, what we *listen to* is God and what we *do* is turn to God, and so intimately are these two aspects of obedience linked that Benedict allows no interval between one and the other. No sooner do we hear the Word than we do it, and it is this that makes obedience perfect. In fact for most of us there often is a gap between the two, and it is this gap that Fr. Borias sees being placed by Benedict between the two liturgies, a gap put there because it is a gap that Christ himself tells us to make when he teaches us to be both simple and prudent. The first liturgy expresses the simplicity of principle, the second expresses the prudence of our practice.

An individual will find it easier than a community to harmonize simplicity and prudence: this is why the constitutions require consultation and voting. The idea isn't to limit the number of guests but to make sure that any welcome offered is truly offered in the name of the entire community, so that all may realize in their heart that epiphany of God manifesting himself equally in themselves as the guest of God and in the stranger as the guest of God. If such a gap is put between hearing and doing, it is because there is such divine beauty in the monastic ideal of hospitality that we must go out of our way to live it ceaselessly.

Persons who offer hospitality must know how to make themselves available to the one they welcome. Since each individual has a different temperament, there is the problem of a monk being too busy to be hospitable, there are the problems that are caused if a monk is the sort of person who is too ready to talk, too suspicious about other people, too anxious to impress, too much in need of some escape—we have in fact a whole range of human failings that stifle our hearts and minds, that empty our welcome and make it meaningless, that reduce it to a sham. But other things will also affect our hospitality: like being a listed building, or the geographical facts we can't escape. Town monasteries always tend to be cheap hotels, and country monasteries are tourist attractions; if your monastery achieves some academic, musical, or other distinction, you can expect the flow of specialists to start any time; if you are near the main road, then you have to expect tramps; if you are out in the desert, you can be sure that the next new road will be planned to go near the monastery. In fact, it won't matter what sort of monastery you are or where you are built; there will always be guests just as there were in the time of Benedict. This doesn't mean there won't be any problems (Sundays, for instance, won't be a day of rest), but there will be problems that we can do our best to meet. If a guest wants to go to confession and no priest is available, then let one of the monks (or nuns) be available so the guest will at least "hear the Word of God from one of the seniors," meaning someone who is senior in wisdom rather than by age or profession. Or again, the perpetual problem of the effect our shops have on visitors, tourists, and guests, and whether there is any intrinsic or spiritual value in the things we make available. Obviously, these shops are meant to be an exchange of services between monastery and public, though how best that is done can never be easy to decide.

Let us return to the problem of closing the gap between hearing and doing, between simplicity and prudence, between guest and myself. The surest way to a solution must lie in understanding what constitutes a "meeting"—whether between God and human or between human and human, that is, in understanding how liberty turns an encounter into a meeting with a welcome, since without that liberty there can be no true hospitality, no talk of Christ being manifest in the guest, no awareness of monk and guest being part of the way God is gathering his people together.

To ensure this liberty, Benedict combines humanity and faith: the humanity by which we treat a human as human and the faith by which we treat God as God. Unless we treat a guest with all the respect due to a human being and in the faith that God is manifest in this encounter, our hospitality will not be monastic. We need to remember that all travelers, whether on foot or flying by jet, are disoriented and dislocated. Health, hygiene, habits, mental composure, all need to be met with understanding, or the new arrival will feel himself inferior to the host and inferior to his own usual self. But the monk, too, has an equilibrium and rhythm in his way of life, and unless he can present himself in his own character as a monk, he can be of no value to the guest. Benedict wants each to be himself so that the encounter will be a gain for each and not a despiritualizing experience.

This shows how even at the level of *humanitas* there must be this liberty to effect the balance between simplicity and prudence. I've never been guestmaster in my own abbey, but I can see why Benedict wants the guestmaster to be something of a specialist. A certain wisdom is necessary for hospitality to be fruitful, but learning how to be prudent as well as simple is one way we learn how to put up with everything, including insults offered to Christ. In Scripture the dove is both the type of simplicity and the symbol of the Holy Spirit because simplicity is our Christian awareness that God is present, knowing all, and caring for all. Prudence, on the other hand, means that we are able to be simple without being simpletons, and especially as regards the identity of Christ. When Benedict says the *pax* shouldn't be given to those who don't share our faith in Christ, is he telling us to restrict our offer of monastic hospitality? What then of the many guests who don't share our faith, who may never even have heard of Jesus? To begin with, they are certainly our brothers and sisters, and as such we offer them more than our bare *humanitas;* but then they will often be far nearer the kingdom than we might ever suspect. On the other hand, the communion we do have with them isn't ever going to mature if we start preaching at them the moment they arrive. This is the prudence the gospel expects us to observe, and we can even see its results in the way non-Christians often return to stay with us again and again.

These are all ways in which we can come to see the true value of liberty as the key to authentic hospitality, the key that opens the gate of heaven, which is a title of Our Lady, since she is the most hospitable of all created beings, and the one who, through listening to the Word and performing it, is the one who has the greatest liberty.

3. The Monastery as Our Home

The Benedictine vision of Christ knocking at the door of the monastery has the divine beauty that makes us realize that our monastery is the house of God, while the double liberty of being human and Christian helps us to see the monastery as the earthly home of humans seeking the liberty that is essential if we are to hear God and obey him through offering hospitality to anyone he sends: pagans, tramps, rogues, unbelievers, etc. By sending them, God himself offers us that liberty which we are seeking. In this way guests have a most important part to play in our *conversio,* a point Benedict underlines when he remarks that long-staying guests are in an excellent position to make comments that will either help the abbot in his own search for God or suggest improvements that could be made. There are probably very few monks who haven't at some time learned something helpful from a guest. This is perfectly normal. If Christ has been received, the Word will bear fruit.

When I am a guest in a monastery I always listen to the bidding prayers at their liturgy, and I have always been deeply impressed by the extent to which communities are really praying for others in the presence of God. On one occasion I heard a guest suggest that the monks also ask their guests to pray for the community, and he was perfectly right. After all, our profession is made in public and so our *conversio* can't be just our own private affair; it is something that concerns the whole Church, and the prayer of the guest for us is as valuable and necessary as our prayers for him. Indeed, we have to rely on the Church for our *conversio* just as much as the Church relies on us for the *conversio* of all Christians. This is one way we can add a flavor of simple communal love to our practice of monastic hospitality.

Every meeting with someone else means the death of a particular me and the birth of a new and truer one. To think about this can never be a waste of time. It is even true of all the meetings that have ever gone to make up human history, and it is true of that meeting of all things in Christ. This is why every Benedictine should be ceaselessly engaged in forming, through his ceaseless intimacy with God, a personal capacity to offer others that hospitality without which we face the terrible alternative of self-centeredness. Pentecost, which is the occasion for this letter, is a moment particularly marked by the two movements of recollection and hospitality. For those of us who are overly prompt in answering the bell, it is a time to consider the risks of welcoming a guest to a house deserted by God; and for those who are happier when the house is empty of guests, a time to consider if Christ is truly with them behind their locked doors. Whichever group we belong to, we must either present ourselves in our character as monks or we shall be accused of misleading both the Church and the world.

Many thanks indeed to all who have ever offered hospitality to the temporary guest who signs himself

Denis Huerre, *Abbot-president*
Congregation of Subiaco
Sant' Ambrogio, Rome

Epiphany 1985

On "Adoratio" and "Conversio"

To All Members of the Congregation:

An interesting way to have shaped this Epiphany letter would have been to concentrate on a problem that three members of the congregation seem to feel about the relation of *conversio* to *adoratio:* one raised the question with regard to Benedict at Subiaco; one with regard both to his own interiorization and to his surprise when a confrère showed himself to be unaware of the need either for *conversio* or *adoratio,* though it wasn't clear if this was due to the common problem of practicing adoration or to some intellectual difficulties in grasping the nature of these two aspects of our life.

Rather than dealing with these specific and personal questions separately, I shall try to set out my own perceptions of the role that adoration has in the Rule. Communities I have visited will recognize a lot of what I say, but it bears repeating, since this concerns the fundamentals to be reflected upon in our daily life. I say this because the three things I see to be essential to our daily life are not only essential to true living adoration but are also the three things that, taken together, sum up the teachings of Benedict:

1) The monastic life is the life of someone who is *monos,* or solitary.
2) The life of a Benedictine is that of a cenobite, forming part of a *koinōnia,* to use the Greek word Benedict translates as *societas* (society).
3) The life of a human being is one that is fulfilled only by the interior progress of *conversio.*

I will consider three aspects of our life and examine how and why each implies *adoratio.* I hope also to show how the gospel brings together all these strands in the figure of the publican, which Benedict selects as the highest example of *adoratio,* the perfection of which is the monastic path of salvation.

1. Adoration and Solitude

The first step to adoration is away from the "many words" of idolators, away from their *multiloquio* toward the "soberness" (*nepsis*) or "few-ness of words," which Benedict indicates to be the opposite of the chattering world of gossip that we must leave behind through *conversio* as we search for that ideal of speaking to God with a single phrase—even better, with a single word—in which we include every shade of truth about ourselves, about the center of our being, person, and conscience. To do this is to confess our essential uniqueness or solitude, not in being ashamed of ourselves and groveling in self-abasement, but in accepting the one fact that confers a true nobility upon each of us, accepting the fact that makes each of us more than just a faceless number or part of a herd. Each of us does have a number that is our rank in the community as provided by the Rule, but our uniqueness, solitude, our singularity is expressed not in that number but in the *name* that is proper to each of us, a name that is always respected, since it indicates that each of us is a unique face of God. A name is more than just a convenient label tied to an individual; it expresses the beauty of our solitude and uniqueness that is a privilege—one that can never be taken from us. Each of our names signifies everything each of us is; it contains in itself the whole of our personal histories and destinies, our pasts and our futures.

When we hear the name of someone we like, our reaction isn't likely to be an act of adoration. If we are normal and not in the grip of some current collective enthusiasm, when we name a person, what we are doing is calling up, in one word, a whole list of associations, only some of which may be pleasant. Our own name is just such a word and one that implies just such a list, a list that we ought to study, though it takes a certain amount of courage for us to do this. Until we have made that list, we can never honestly know the truth of what we really are. Once we have made that list and studied it, we find ourselves freed from self-adulation; and it is this freedom that makes adoration possible, that makes possible for us to say in prayer, "I adore you in spite of that list, and I adore you because of that list," for if we adore God, it must be both *above* all else and *in* all else.

a. Adoring God Above All

Every day we see something added to that list of what in fact we truly are: it is a list that includes all our qualities, our faults, our autobiography, our history as part of a family, as part of our society. It includes all the things—whether we are proud of them or not—that we must face and accept and integrate, though we must do this only with the aim of leaving all that behind and finding ourselves free to adore the One who is beyond everything, beyond self and beyond others, infinitely beyond anything whatsoever in creation. This is what Benedict is speaking about when he uses the word "preference;" it is what the Gospels mean when speaking about sacrificing all for the sake of the treasure we have found, and what Paul means when he speaks of considering all as nothing for the sake of God.

In practice, once we have focused on the goal, we move toward it gradually, and our first step is taken when we create a distance between ourselves and everything that isn't God. In nontheological terms, every human being who becomes aware of his or her personal autonomy will see the need for growing out of the dependence that is normal for a child and will "prefer" that autonomy to any form of reliance that threatens to destroy it.

The word "adoration" is meaningless until we accept this solitude or autonomy. Until we enter it and are able to remain in it, we are not fully human. To stop grasping self means that first we must realize we *have* been grasping it. To abandon self for the sake of others means that first we must have descended into our heart where, as Gregory says of Benedict, we become enlarged and find the freedom that can express itself only by saying to God, "I adore you beyond all things." This relation between self and God is something hidden, but it is not a secret from which others are excluded, since preferring God to all else means that all things are included in that relationship, which only exists because of them, and which is hidden only because it is the distance between self and others created by adoration.

b. Adoring God in All

This is essential to balance and complete what we have just been saying. The possibility of preferring God to all things (which is the definition of true living adoration) will only destroy itself the moment we allow the distance between ourselves and others to become a distance caused by putting ourselves *above* all others, believing we are better than they are. This is a terribly insidious danger that reduces life and produces death and so makes itself the opposite of true *living* adoration. To put a distance between ourselves and all that is not God can all too easily lead us to fabricate a gulf between ourselves and the rest of creation, which makes it the opposite of *true* living adoration. In the Rule, Benedict has found a way of guarding against this by speaking of our encounter with God who is already there, saying *adsum* before we speak, and who is there precisely because there never can be a gulf between ourselves and the rest of God's creation. We can never be other than part of that creation in which God is perpetually present, since it is he who is perpetually creating it. We adore God only *because* he is perpetually creating us and perpetually present in us and perpetually creating our life; only because we can truthfully say, "I adore you because you are my life that is ceaselessly coming from you." This is the one thing we can never say except to God. Children become adult and achieve freedom when they realize that though two people are their parents, it is God who is their origin, and for this reason it would never be possible to address Psalm 138 to our ancestors, family, friends, or contemporaries; it is the reason Jewish commentators make it par excellence the psalm of Adam, that is, the psalm of the human race as contained in its point of origin. Each of us was present in potency at that point, and so Père Beauchamp is able to urge us to locate that point of origin in our own selves. To find that point in our own lives is to find the moment of true adoration, the moment of true awareness that second-by-second we are receiving our lives, our existence from the hand of God. At such a moment of awareness, adoration becomes something totally personal, something that puts us into intimate contact with God *through* Christ *in* the Holy Spirit, a contact that reflects three moments in the life of Jesus that show us the link between solitude and adoration:

    a. His meeting with Nicodemus (rebirth from above);
    b. His meeting with the Samaritan woman (rebirth of consciousness);
    c. The night of Easter (rebirth in resurrection).

We see the same intimate contact with God reflected in the way Paul begins his letters to the Christians of Corinth, Colossus, and Ephesus; in the wording that begins the letter to Jewish Christians; in the wording John uses at the beginning of his Gospel. All these express the same mystery: Christ is found only when we find him already present not only in ourselves but in everything that forms part of God's creation. This is the mystery by which the "self" of each created thing (its dependence on that which is not itself) is the foundation of its praise, its adoration of the creator. This is the mystery that means each of us can be aware that our solitude, our uniqueness, is the result of a personal act of the Word who became flesh.

But then also, if we are to adore the Father, we are to do so in *spirit*. In his letter to the Christians of Rome, Paul devotes the whole of chapter 8 to explaining how it is through the union of our spirit and the Holy Spirit that the mutual relationship between oneself and God is perfected. This "personalization" (so to speak) of the Christian life is something we find manifested everywhere, from the individual characteristics of the four evangelists to the way John of the Cross and Teresa of Avila speak of the Holy Spirit. The number of human beings is the number of ways there are of being a follower of Christ, of being a Christian. When I realize this, I realize how wrong I was as a child to think that heaven would be boring. It is true that God will be the all-that-is, but each will always retain his or her uniqueness, because that solitude of each as unique is what adoration needs, and it can never be destroyed in the communion of saints.

2. Adoration and Community

The essential meaning of "cenobite" is "oneness with others" or "communing with others"; but such unity is not only a *result* of being in communion with others; it is also created by communion with them. If we understand it from both sides in this way, then—as I see it—it expresses an ideal that cannot be surpassed, an ideal that is brought out by de Lubac in his commentary on the conciliar document *Dei Verbum,* which opens with the first words of the First Epistle of John, words that, as de Lubac points out, summarize the whole of Christian revelation by telling us its subject, its author, and its method. Speaking to cenobites, Benedict conveys what John has summarized when he gives us his teaching on the triple *koinōnia:* the communion between Father and Son to which the apostles bore united witness, thus begetting that communion between themselves and the Son, which in turn begat communion between all the faithful, and so between each member of that tiny group of the faithful that we call our monastery. Such communion ensures that we in our community are a present manifestation of that original apostolic communion with Christ through which we have such a direct share in the eternal communion between the three persons of the Trinity. The mutual love of the three divine persons hears its echo in the perfection of our adoration that has its roots in the communion of our own monastic community.

On the one hand, we can see how such adoration—based as it is in such communion—confirms what we have already said about adoration needing solitude, since communion is possible between humans only because each of them is unique, each is a sole individual capable of solitude; there can be no communion except between persons who remain what they are without fear of dissolving into the faceless anonymity of an impersonal crowd. On the other hand, we can see this also confirms what we said about solitude and uniqueness being the most noble part of a human person, provided it is nourished by communication with others, so that it doesn't wither into the isolation that results from creating a gulf between myself and others. Anyone who creates such a gulf reduces himself or herself to a caricature of the ideal self-giving person. Isolated in this way, you live for yourself alone and become like the only survivor of a group who still insists on the group's right to self-determination.

To call oneself a follower of Christ is to identify oneself with the community Christ founded: a hermit is fully aware that he is a member of this community, because his spiritual warfare is against the temptation of becoming isolated at heart; or (in other words) his path is that of persistent awareness of the presence of God, the Only Lover of All Humanity, who manifests himself in the uniqueness of Christ, the Only Begotten.

To be perpetually aware of the presence of God is to be perpetually aware of his glory, and it is this awareness that makes every word and every gesture (all that we say and do) an act of adoration. Benedict makes this clear when he speaks of the glory of God and shows that for himself—as for St. John—adoration and community are inseparable because each implies the other.

The Rule affirms this by teaching the following:

a. The community rises together to adore the Holy Trinity.
b. We adore God in the novice and guest; the manifestation of divine compassion is God's glory.
c. We are to glorify God and adore him through our commercialization and all our money-making activities.

In these teachings Benedict indicates that the solitude of each individual member of our community bears its fruit in the communal joy of fraternal communion, in the joy of the apostles, and in the communion of all the faithful; in the joy of seeing the Lord who had been rejected by humans now acknowledged and recognized, celebrated and welcomed. Such Easter joy we learn from John.

To see that the phrase "beyond all and in all" is appropriate when speaking of adoration with regard to solitude is to see that it is equally appropriate with regard to community. We adore God *beyond* all because it is through hope (without being discouraged by the length of the journey) that we all advance together toward the day when all will be united; we adore God *in* all because he is the living origin of all, the One who is perpetually creating all, the One that Jesus has told us to call collectively "*our* Father." And since we are baptized not only in the name of that Father and of Jesus his son but also in the name of the Holy Spirit, it is in the Spirit that we are able, as was Jesus, to call God our Father.

3. "Adoratio" and "Conversio"

The most fundamental inquiry a human being can initiate involves the origin and destiny of our race. The most fundamental resolution to that inquiry is adoration, though only provided that we understand adoration in a double sense, that is, as referring both to the solitude of each of us as a single, unique individual being, and to the fulfilment that each of us can find only in that solidarity which allows us to include other individuals in that word "us" and allows us to refer to God as "*our* Father." If we understand how adoration has this double perspective—how it prevents any celebration of God that fails to celebrate the harmony between the divine uncreated and his human creation—then every act of adoration becomes a source of harmony between all members of the human race.

At first glance that may seem a little oversimplified, as in fact it is, until we balance it with an understanding of what exactly it is—*in* us and *among* us—that prevents and denies adoration. This, the exact opposite of adoration, is what we call "evil," and the "problem of evil" as usually stated in the question "How can we worship in spirit and in truth the God who, in his creation, allows a place for evil and for the suffering of the innocent?"

To answer the question conceived in these terms involves finding the point from which evil and adoration could be seen side by side and compared with each other. Putting the problem in this way is simply to ask what our chances are of persuading God, of cajoling him or flattering him; and that is exactly how we turn religion into idolatry.

As monks and nuns we should be aware of what the problems are that evil creates both in our own selves and in our relationship with others. It may be that what bothered the third member of our congregation, to whom I referred at the beginning of this letter, was whether adoration could do any good, whether conversion was worthwhile; if so, it may have been the result of his awareness of this problem of evil. If that is the case, then what we need to see is how this presence, this possibility, of evil is what links adoration and conversion, though particularly so when evil is the rejection and denial we call "sin." Adoration without conversion is either sheer adulation or a mere emotional reaction of happiness due to some fleeting perception of beauty or harmony. True adoration is never directed to anything of that sort, but only to the divine Beauty that is the source of all that is beautiful which, because it is that source, is what we seek, though we know it can never be found without struggle and without devoting a whole lifetime to the search. Because this is the case, our search is most often successful only in old age, since our progress in this adoration of the divine Beauty can never go faster than our progress in the slow work of conversion; indeed, each step in our conversion is a manifestation of truth only insofar as it advances us to a truer adoration of God. Without adoration, *conversio* would be nothing more than progress in self-will.

A letter like this is clearly not the place to enter into all the ramifications of evil in general, but it may help some of you if we glance at a specifically monastic form of evil that we can best approach by stating two things every community must avoid if it is to make any progress toward the goal of perfect adoration:

a. Our goal must never be defined as *either* solitude *or* community: the goal must always be seen as both, and each must always be approached through the other; first, because this is the only way we can harmonize the alternatives that seem so disparate; second, because this harmony alone is what constitutes the source from which adoration can flow. How the two can be harmonized, how each goal can be realized through the other, is what each community must teach itself.

b. This goal (this harmony of the double goal that each community must have) can never be centered *on* or *in* the community itself; our aim must always be to link the community to the wider Church, to the entire human race. Any failure here can only end in a community that adores itself.

Nor can a letter like this enter with any fullness into the problem of converting evil into good; yet with regard to this there is one point I would like to emphasize before ending this section. The wisdom of Benedict has ensured that the Rule is an excellent weapon for avoiding all those multiple banes occasioned by false gnosticism, a persistent temptation that crops up century after century. We can think of (1) the temptation to imagine salvation as nothing but a matter of belonging to a small elite who have true intellectual light; or (2) we can be tempted by the millennarian's fantasy of good and evil as two divine absolutes at war with each other so that "the present" is never more than a point from which we can look forward a thousand years to a victory for the good that will establish a kingdom of the spirit here on earth; or (3) it prompts us toward an asceticism dictated by views that see all matter (that see anything, like the body, which is material) as something evil; or (4) it can even prompt us toward some of those views that fail to see Christ as the one and only mediator between creator and creation, views that posit endless *intermediaries* between heaven and earth, and who are not the same thing as a *mediator*.

These are speculations popularly associated with the later members of the congregation founded by Bl. Joachim of Floris (d. 1202) but against which we are protected by a Rule that offers Christ as the sole remedy for our evil and sin, that offers us Christ as what we are to "prefer above all things." There is no need to be surprised that the world of miracles and marvels is missing from the Rule; for Benedict there is only the one marvel—who is Christ; for Benedict the only miracle is our stability in adoration.

4. Appendix: The Publican and the Benedictine

The one passage in Luke's Gospel that conveys to me the same sort of paradox and spiritual freshness as the Beatitudes is where Christ teaches through the parable of the publican, a parable that teaches the follower of Christ to know that he is in the presence of God and so to admit that he is a sinner; a parable that teaches the Benedictine how to reach the perfect love of God, which leaves behind us every trace of fear, which teaches us both how we are raised (as Luke says) to the state of justification or holiness, and how we are raised (as Benedict puts it) above ourselves, filled with that ease of freedom from self that opens to us the life of true adoration.

Every time I hear Benedict tell me that no matter where a monk is— oratory, monastery, road, or field—no matter whether he is sitting, standing, or walking, he is to make this confession of God who alone can save—I am reminded of the Shema: "Listen, Israel, you are to love the Lord your God with all your heart, all your being, all your strength; and remember the words of this commandment I have given you today: keep them ever-present in your heart, repeat them to your sons, and repeat them ceaselessly to yourselves no matter whether you are at home or on the road, whether you are lying down or standing up."

Here we see what adoration really is and why it demands the three elements of solitude, community, and conversion; why it is that different monks at different times will find one of the three predominating, and why it is that the true monk in his solitude is always of necessity in communion with others, since his uniqueness and his oneness with others are the two sides bordering his slow path to conversion, along which we become aware, like the publican, that we are never worthy of adoring God and yet, like him, are always aware that God is calling us to adore him ceaselessly, both in the hidden solitude of our heart and in our own community of cenobites: in the two places where "the Father knows."

Denis Huerre, *Abbot-president*
Congregation of Subiaco
Sant' Ambrogio, Rome

On Monastic Asceticism

To All Members of the Congregation:

This isn't going to be a handbook on the subject but only a letter about it: I might have found a better title, but I have kept to this one for two reasons: 1) In 1982 an abbot of our congregation wrote: "People today feel 'worried' about their sins, about 'moving in the wrong direction,' but they don't *weep* for them, and yet compunction is at the root of monastic spirituality in the whole of our tradition from the Desert Fathers to Abbot Marmion. Is anxiety just the modern form of compunction?" 2) More recently a doctor interested in the relation between health and holiness wrote to me in 1984 about the importance Benedictines give the body in monastic life. I have kept the title "Monastic Asceticism," as it seemed to cover both topics while I reflected on them.

Asceticism (as Christians have always understood the term) is a warfare that aims at victory for the believer; a progress of the whole being toward unity with God that will bring us closer to unity with all beings; in it we are exercising our hope for the salvation that we desire and that we receive from Christ. To live the ascetic life is to aim at removing all the obstacles we think of collectively as "evil" (or as being at least an evil as far as we are concerned, since our aim is for ourselves to emerge victorious from the battle).

This victory, being saved from defeat, is something we can still call both health and holiness: *salus,* as Marrou says, is how the Roman peasant referred to bodily health, and the word was taken up by Christian writers to mean spiritual health; both senses mean "saved" from death, much as we say in English "safe and sound" (and the same connection exists between "all-hallows" and being "hale and hearty," or "sain et sauf" in French, etc.).

So this letter is about things like anguish, health, safety, salvation, as well as asceticism. The three sections will consider:

1) If anguish has a place in monastic asceticism;
2) What place our body has in this asceticism;
3) How the Word of God is the key to monastic asceticism.

1. Anxiety or Stress

Everybody knows what it is to feel anxious, and indeed we can't reach a state of peace without having experienced it. But the way you experience it will depend on the type of person you are, whether you tend to be over-confident or always uncertain of yourself. The state of peace isn't a psycho-logical state you reach by becoming less aggressive or feeling more self-confidence, though the anxieties that beset us on the way can be caused by lack of decision, fear of letting your heart open, fear of having to squeeze through the narrow door, and all sorts of anxieties colored by upbringing and personal history.

All this is fairly obvious, and the only point I want to emphasize is that there's a great temptation these days to oversimplify by blaming stress on the modern pace of life in big cities. Anxiety is much older than city life and can be provoked by worry about bad weather, attacks by a hostile tribe, and by all the other calamities we can't control. People who blame modern life in the collective herd aren't going to escape stress in community life. Some have asked for dispensations because they found the stress of living with a hundred others intolerable; others, because they found the same living with only five. Both types include those who suffer real anguish because they imagine themselves victimized by the rest. Interior grace can't be put on like a monastic habit, and there are many community members who may look calm and unruffled to others but are in a perpetual state of inner stress.

If you happen to be startled by someone or frightened by something, that is one sort of stress, but it doesn't last long. If you feel slighted, in-sulted, or despised by someone, that is another sort of anxiety and much deeper, but people get over it after a bit. Some people are in a state of per-petual panic and stage fright, but even that isn't the same as deep-seated inner stress, and this is because asceticism isn't the same as just learning to live in a community without losing your patience and becoming a ner-vous wreck. Anxieties arise in the heart, and that is where asceticism is to be practiced. It is here that the two are interconnected, at this "wounded" center of our being (the wound indicated by the phrase "tears of compunc-tion"). Let's look a bit closer at both the point in us and the point of time, the point where and when anxiety and asceticism meet. This heart or place is the deepest center of our self, the precious center of our life, which con-stitutes our liberty and freedom, and which is our dignity as human beings and our likeness to God as images of God.

Worry, stress, and anxiety are results of losing that liberty, but espe-cially when this is caused by *using* the liberty we have in order to *misuse* it, by using liberty to extinguish itself, since liberty is a certain fire which should burn in us to be a lamp for the path (which is the way we live our

individual lives) and which should be able to set others on fire. Asceticism
is how we relight that fire so that it becomes contagious, and so that we
can sing the Beatitudes, and so that we can celebrate the beatitude and bliss
of liberty in Christ (Romans 8).

Asceticism must come face to face with anxiety if it is to be victorious,
and (as is commonly taught in monasteries) it does so in two phases:

a. Listening to what is being said by one's own intelligence and will,
by one's awareness, memory, and imagination of things, and listening to
what is being *said* there *in* oneself *about* oneself. This is the sort of recollection that helps one's descent into the center, and in a more serious way
than is meant by the rather unspecial sort of "examination of conscience"
that often lasts no more than the space of an Our Father. This deep recollection is how we come to realize both the beauty and the malice of our own
thoughts. This is a first stage in "knowing oneself," and it leads to much
clearing of the inner fog where people are generally happy to let their inner
life remain stagnated. Thousands of our little anxieties disappear with that
fog.

b. Having cleared the fog, our heart can be allowed to open as we come
to realize that this is the secret place where our superficiality has prevented
us from knowing ourselves, that inner self-ignorance we become aware of
only if it disguises itself in the form of anxieties. We realize that by turning
to whichever of the many forms of outerness we prefer, the effect has been
to close up our innerness, deprive it of speech, and force it to communicate through these worries, anxieties, and neuroses. Our descent to the inner is what makes it easier to speak about ourselves, even if only to ourselves.

First the prodigal son "came to himself" and then he decided "I shall
go to him and say. . ."; the consequence is that the son is forgiven and
clothed. The moment we open our hearts, God removes the veil that was
concealing the liberty we always had. Benedict mentions this lack of any
real interval between the opening and the unveiling at the end of chapter 7.
It is God whom we find present by opening (the "adsum" we hear upon
knocking) that eliminates the anxieties so that we can move forward on the
path.

Descent to the heart followed by the opening (opening to the spiritual
father, to the whole community) are the two stages that have cured many
victims of stress. It raises the question as to how far a community can follow the same path of descent to itself so that as a community it can come
to understand the things in its corporate personality that hinder or help
the ease with which members relate to each other. Outside the monastery,
people suffering from stress seem to be drowning in the great sea of humanity and the tide of events. An individual in the monastery can often
feel exactly the same way. The worst sort of herd instinct that can happen

in a monastic community is a collective loss of liberty that can crush individuals under the weight of a collective neurosis so that no member ever gets a chance to "know himself" through this descent. We have to be careful that this sort of thing doesn't happen. Our vocation is to the community, not to a collective, for a collective can do no wrong, since it eliminates all sense of personal liberty and initiative.

2. Monastic Asceticism and the Body

Anxieties are tangles and knots at the deep center, and these affect the body. How the mind affects the body and how the body reacts through emotions to what is in the mind are well known, and what follows will be three reflections on this:

a. We all (eventually) have need of the infirmarian, as Benedict saw; the infirmary (including visits to the dentist, surgery, and hospital) is as necessary as the kitchen. A European health service official told me that he thought some religious communities of brothers and sisters probably had a rather childlike belief in what advertisements claimed for pills and things, took them in large quantities, and charged them to their national health service. It's hard to say which is more naive: thinking quack remedies can cure you or thinking you can cure yourself without some elementary knowledge of health and hygiene. There used to be quite a tradition, not long ago, of how virtuous it was for nuns and monks to entrust their health to the infirmarian, even to the superior, while looking forward to the early death this so often entailed. On the whole, I think I find this holy indifference preferable to the egotism that shows itself in people who perpetually dose themselves to look after their health.

Put that way, it leads us to rethink what St. Benedict says about fulfilling the commands of superiors, because what he is saying in fact is that merely to do it, merely to carry it out, is worth nothing unless it is performed in the liberty that requires our free consent at the deep center of the heart, a consent that we give because it is being seen as the command given by God through the superior, a consent that means we are consenting as Catholics to what our human nature is. God has invented the sort of human being we are; what does he want from this invention? What can we do about it?

b. God having made us the way we are, what does the body mean to us? How important should it be to us? The first thing to make clear is that we cannot answer such questions unless we think of ourselves as living human beings, not bits of things stuck together, whether we talk of two things (body and mind) or three things (mind, body, heart). We aren't an assembly of parts but integral units or entities. There cannot be a true spirituality unless it expresses the whole of what we are. Benedictines have been celebrated for the equilibrium in which our monasteries keep body and mind, yet there are some tendencies today that seem to forget this and tie labels on monks, e.g., A is a laybrother type, B is an intellectual type, C is an artistic type, etc. What these labels do is deny these people the possibility of developing their other human aspects and becoming that ideal Benedictine that is the balanced human. This may be only a tendency, but it could be very costly to a community that forced people into molds.

c. The third reflection on our "body" is a reminder that this is not at all the same thing that Paul refers to as "flesh." The heart, mind, or deep center is what helps us to live so that "flesh" is constantly being converted into "body" (and the reflection of this inner structure in our brain is something attracting a lot of attention). Another "element" of this structure would be our sexuality, since (at least in the West) we are not awfully good at integrating sexuality with heart, sexuality with spirit, sexuality with body. Instead of integrating it, we treat it as something special or separate, and the result is that we become lopsided, we simply can't see that sexuality is a matter of our whole being, reflected in everything that is human. As a result, there is an alternative way of evading this essential aspect of being human, and that is to pretend we are angels—and that is simply another form of inhumanity. The alternatives we seem to choose are either being obsessed by sex or pretending we are angels: both are obstacles to the conversion of "flesh" into "body," and both tend to degrade "body" to its fragile reality as "flesh," which is so short-lived that it needs constant intakes of food to ensure that its constituent cells are incessantly replaced. This alone is an indication of how dangerous it is to allow health (which is proper to our human condition) to disintegrate so that we imagine there is a choice between *either* health of body *or* health of mind. In referring to "flesh," Benedict restricts himself to mentioning its ambiguous desires and how easy it is for its slaves to go astray. In referring to "body," the most important thing he says is in the passage where he reconstructs the ladder of Jacob as the ladder leading from monk to God. The rungs are our daily acts that link the sides which are body and mind, and all three elements are essential for our ascent.

The consequences of this teaching on monastic asceticism can't be summed up in a few words, but here I want to add a note on body and stress. Flesh needs conversion into body; what *angst* needs converting into is "fear of God." Anxiety is irrational, the fear of God is eminently rational—just as we can have excellent reasons for human fear that this or that might happen, so the fear of God has to be based on reason. Fear of God isn't being frightened by a superman; God is totally present in us and totally aware of what we are, but he doesn't observe us with detachment, since his concern is with the way we use our liberty, and this we know from what Jesus has taught us. Fright can paralyze us and make us behave like children; fear is that reverence for God by which we become his children, his brothers and sisters. The goal of monastic asceticism is our rebirth in the spirit.

3. Asceticism and the Holy Spirit

Christianity and Christian monasticism avoid the opposites of activism and quietism; yet each can seem tempting to a monk. This is especially true of an attitude that sees monastic stability not as the faith of living fidelity but as a noble stoicism of endurance that puts up with things at all costs. What Benedict teaches is the spiritual art of life, the art of living spiritually, not a science of spiritual techniques. An art of the spiritual life has to be an actual living of that life in the Spirit.

By activism or voluntarism one means the sort of way some people interpret the asceticism taught by Confucius. Difficulties were raised at the profession of a young Chinese who was able to say (like George Washington) that he had never told a lie and that such a thing would be unthinkable for the Confucian tradition in which he had been brought up. He was asked if he had been attracted to the Church merely as something that offered even stricter ideals or something more loving.

Spiritual warfare isn't fought by mercenaries or by slaves who are being forced to fight; it is fought by free people who rejoice in their freedom. They may be fighting *for* that freedom but, being free, the warfare itself is already a participation in the victory. This is the point that Benedict makes very forcefully when he says that the paschal victory of Christ colors the whole of the preceding Lent with its joy. This joy to which monks look forward in Lent certainly isn't any ordinary sort of jolliness; one can't exactly analyze what makes it special, but we can say it is something to do with the state of being on easy, friendly terms with God, since otherwise there wouldn't be any meaning in the phrase "becoming sons of God," nor any meaning in the title "abbot," which is a title given for no other reason than to make it easier for us to understand God's presence. This is why Benedict takes care to emphasize that the title "abbot" can never be the excuse for a tyranny over the weak. This paschal joy that we anticipate in Lent is our participation in the victory by which Christ the Suffering Servant (or literally "slave") becomes the reigning sovereign. The way we "participate" in this is through our victory over every obstacle to our liberty, so that progressing in this liberty, we progress in the state of being on easy, friendly terms with God.

I find particularly attractive this picture of our being at ease with God as Benedict analyzes it in his section on love and fear: the fear fades but it can never evaporate, while love grows and knows no limit, so the mystery of it isn't of the sort to yield to easy ideas. Psalm 50 celebrates this conversion from sinful liberty into the joy of spiritual health or deliverance, and treats it as though it meant putting one's awareness into a new orbit, leaving the level where the realities are seen in a way that causes regret, and reaching a level where the same realities display the meaning of all I have done in the wider context of my whole life; and I see my life in the even wider context of God's design. This is the moment when every fault, having found its liberator, can be realized as a *felix culpa*.

This can be seen only from a higher level, the one we reach by monastic asceticism, when we see the desirability of Christ, who all the time has been presiding over all the efforts we have been making. Free of the depression in which we could have wallowed had we not raised our eyes to Christ, every element of our being seems to find its proper place at this point we have reached: the *heart* inhabited by a peace that embraces both past and future; the *mind* is no longer tempted to be proud but, knowing things as they really are, has the true pride of being proud of God, of finding true pride in him; the *body* liberated from being flesh, aware that its true value is being human in spite of all its tendency to slip back; to be human because I am human—a being that could never be fully human when bothered and anxious about having to be up to date, a slave to the latest fashion and trendy ideas. To be human means being able to use worldly things without becoming addicted to them, to be able to make use of all five senses as supports for our journey to meet the Son of Man on his return.

Without this sort of spiritual insight into things, asceticism would not be Christian, and the same approach helps to solve thousands of the day-to-day problems that exist in all monasteries: fast days, what to serve at meals (and when to have them—note the evolution of breakfast from frustulum), vigils and the night prayer common to so many ancient and modern communities, the provision of lavatories, showers, and baths, etc. so often inconvenient or lacking in old buildings, whether monastic or not.

In this context one has also to mention the sort of things so often discussed that illustrate our reaction against the artificiality of old-fashioned hieratic views. These include the outer signs of bodily posture and movement in the liturgy, signs of reverence to superiors, deportment, visible signs of distinction between grades and groups in the community. We have different sets of values nowadays and, on the whole, things do seem more natural in our monasteries, with a great deal more of the give and take that makes it easier to live together. Should we be thinking again of how to harmonize the outer with the inner in our life, so that the worship of God in body-mind-heart expresses a better balance between the personal and the communal?

4. Conclusion: The Word and Our Asceticism

The Word of God is what opens our deepest center, and so we can call it the "key" to our asceticism and to our understanding of what asceticism is. The Word is ever asking to enter that heart, and by his consent to that entry, the monk himself becomes a living word. Our own choice determines what the heart-mind-body become, and there are many ways in which that choice is affected by the time and place in which we are living. The ideal asceticism is the one that is aware of those influences when it makes decisions, and yet leads us to a freedom that reflects and expresses the uniqueness that each of us has. What, with the heart closed, would be individualistic and egotistic is converted by the opening of our hearts into the authentic personal uniqueness of our being, singing itself to God. That in brief is the perfection of the opening of heart and lips; the perfection of a path that starts with the confession of sin converting itself into the confession of love for God and neighbor.

This perfection or culmination of the path isn't a point we reach at a certain moment in our life; it has to be the goal of a whole united lifetime until our life has sung the whole of itself to God. And here, as this letter reaches its own end, I would like to quote what the English doctor D. W. Vinicot says about this "ending": "O God, may I be alive when I die." If that prayer is granted, our asceticism will not have been in vain; we shall have reached that true east which, on this gradual path, we had slowly discovered to be the direction we were meant to take.

Denis Huerre, *Abbot-president*
Congregation of Subiaco
Sant' Ambrogio, Rome

Epiphany 1986

"Conversio" and Old Age

Dear Brothers and Sisters of the Subiaco Congregation,

"Monastic theologians and historians have neglected whole areas connected with health and sickness; surely it is time they turned to more specific details, not only about the development of hospitals and nursing homes through the ages but about our approach to such questions as social security and the age of retirement, even though there is so little in the Rule about sickness, old age, and death."

Let's hope that infirmarians and superiors will take note of this appeal that I quote from a letter dated February 20, 1985. Not being any sort of expert on geriatrics, I can only write from the point of view of someone who is already beginning to feel the effects of age, but at least I will not make the mistake of writing about old age as if it were a sort of illness instead of being simply a stage of life, in particular that stage of life when our conversion of heart should become more perfect, since this is the stage of life when we start growing close to our encounter with God. The three aspects of old age and *conversio* that I shall look at will be:

1. Why Benedict Isn't More Forthcoming.
2. The Old Monk Standing Face to Face with God.
3. The Value of the Aged Monk to His Community.

1. Why Benedict Isn't More Forthcoming

Before we can decide why the Rule has so little to say about the old and their death, we must remember that death for Benedict didn't have quite the same sort of tragic quality that it has for some people nowadays. The only real tragedy of death would be for the dialogue we began with God at birth not to continue into eternity: if he says to us "I don't know you" and refuses to open the door because we have turned away from him. This doesn't mean of course that we shouldn't feel any emotion when a good monk dies in the peace of God; on the contrary, it is only right that we should regret the passing of those we have loved. We are certainly going to miss those for whom we have had an affection; we will miss our little chats with them. Sadness at such a time doesn't suggest any lack of faith.

Jesus wept over Lazarus because he loved him, and we, too, have a right to weep even if less publicly. However, let us remember that Jesus was far more upset by the lack of faith shown by friends and neighbors than he was by the tragedy of his friend's death. Benedict's chief concern isn't with how we react to someone else's death but with how we meet God after our own death. If we want a guide as to how we should react to the death of others, we shall find it in the expressions of sorrow and of hope enshrined in the "Office of the Dead" and in the customs of our own monastery.

There is a place where Newman says, "Grace operates with more power in the young than in the old because the young have less to restrain them from practicing virtue. As the Greek poet says, 'Our mind grows stiff with age,' and with their minds as cold as their icy bodies, the old need grace by the bucketful if it's going to warm their heart. This is why I prefer old saints to young ones. If I was daring in my own youth, it was because I was ignorant, but now that I know only too well what it costs to remain that way, I am afraid of the sacrifice." St. Bernard says something similar when he tells Richard of Fountains (Letter 96) that *conversio* is easier for a layman entering a monastery than it is for a tepid monk when he reaches old age. Benedict's concern in the Rule, of course, is different: he wants to describe the ideal old monk, the monk who has grown wise, the true *senex* in his monastery, a master of spiritual discernment, well-fitted to receive guests and train novices. Infected with virtue he is well-fitted to overcome the evil that infects others and so the ideal agent for reconciling the excommunicated and ostracized. Just as Benedict gives us a description of the perfect abbot and perfect cellarer, so he gives us the ideal of a senior monk: Newman and Bernard describe the reality, not the ideal.

It is interesting to note that Bernard was fifty when he wrote to Richard, and Newman was fifty-nine when he described himself as afraid of sacrifice in his old age. Where each of these agrees with Benedict is that none of them suggests that *conversio* is possible *only* when you are young. Whatever one's age and at whatever moment of one's whole life, our attitude should be that of the publican who was justified by that single moment of truth in the heart of his mind.

It is when we notice the absence from the Rule of anything on the fear of dying, on the difficulties even the oldest monks can experience of persevering until death, that we realize Benedict's true aim is to bring us, at the end of life, face to face with God in that attitude which alone constitutes the perfection of *conversio;* for it is *conversio* that enables us to persevere all through whatever remains of our life and on into the beyond.

2. The Old Monk Standing Face to Face with God

Here I don't propose to talk about cases of senility (and still less of those sadder cases of premature senility) but about the *senex* or old monk who remains lively and often deceptively youthful as he approaches his coming encounter with God. What is it that God expects from this encounter?

In the first place, God expects the aged nun or monk to become ever more what the word "professed" actually means. The word is cognate with "prophet," meaning not a foreteller through revelation of the future but one who receives that revelation made by God through Christ, through the Christ revealed in the New Testament as living, as the one through whom we are saved. Like Simeon, the old monk has as his task the handing on of this revelation, a task he can perform with ever greater conviction the more his own energies decline and the less he remains prone to the delusions of self-will. When his life ends, the old monk, too, will be able to say (and often he says it with memorable gracefulness) "Now I can depart, for I am now in peace: I know that he lives."

What God is also wanting of the aged monk is that he should be manifestly waiting for Christ. In some cases it happens that when the cell of a monk recently dead is being tidied, many of the things he has carefully preserved because they might be needed one day turn out to be of no use to any one else in the community; on the other hand, it can happen that the dead monk's cell is already practically bare. In saying this I don't want to give the impression that any importance attaches to the number of things one leaves behind, because the only thing that does matter is whether a monk manifestly prefers Christ to all things, for it is this that shows him to have received the gift of "spiritual preference"—the gift that allows one to grasp our tools, whatever they are, in a way that produces whatever it is for the glory of God, but that also allows one to relinquish them and to relinquish everything, so as to hold oneself ready and detached, purged of all self-centeredness; it is only when Christ is at our center, filling it, that we are saved.

The opposite of the monk whose self-centeredness has been purged is the one who insists on controlling things and people right up to the end; and here I don't mean the sick monks (not necessarily old ones) who like being the center of attention—illness can excuse a lot—but if I start talking about that I shall get diverted from the subject of old age, which must never be treated as if it were a disease or sickness. Indeed, as far as the old monks who have reached a high degree of selflessness are concerned, their old age is a positive benefit to the community, a reminder that Christ, through them, is actually helping us to do his work in the new world that is being born from day to day. As we grow old, the young are constantly renewing the world. To grow old is the way we contribute to the continual birth of the new, to the continual arrival of the future in which we must never fail to see Christ occupying its center. By preferring Christ to all things, we are there with him at that center of the future; at that moment it approaches us to become our present; we are with him in the ceaselessly arriving present, and being with him in this way, we discover that we have found the proper way of getting on in years and growing old.

Let us turn to a final aspect of how the old face God, and one that may not prove as obvious as at first it seems. When we are born, we can expect to face a normal development from child to adult, beginning at the stage when we are called "infant"—that is *in-fans* or not-speaking, a word exactly contrary to *pro-fessus* and *pro-pheta*. This is the first stage of our education, and it ends when we are able to speak, able to produce words with our mouths that can be heard by others and to produce words in our mind that no one else can hear. This is such a usual, normal thing that we can actually forget how utterly extraordinary and miraculous is this power of speech, of language, of being able to communicate the silent speech of our mind to others, to convey to them not just what we seem to be to them in their sight, but what we actually are; to convey our inner personality in a way that means they know us better than they would if they had to depend on the shape of our body or the color of our eyes.

We grow, then, from the stages of babbling and baby talk to the stage of speaking properly; and it is only when we reach this stage that we acquire our true inner freedom, the liberty to say who we truly are and thus to enter the stage of adulthood; then we have reached the stage when people not only know how to defend life and enrich it but, when becoming parents, actually transmit it.

Now life can be received, lived, and transmitted in many different ways, even by the celibate; but what distinguishes human life is what makes its transmission different from animal procreation and is what makes it a mystery and gives it dignity. This is true even if we take life in its wider sense and consider the reception, use, and development of our talents; for when we reach the age of parenthood, there are many ways in which we can give birth, many ways of making our contribution to the human world. Yet this creative, generative phase of our life can wane. Its powers are inherently transitory and, however paradoxical it may seem, I propose to call the third stage that follows from baby and adult the "age of the son"; that, is a label, though, that might seem obviously available only to Christians. Yet I think others will understand me when I say that it is in terms of one's "sonship" rather than one's parenthood that we can best define an individual. Primarily, this is because it is as offspring that we experience the basic mystery of being human, for no one has ever asked to be born; and yet, because the act of becoming a parent is something we consent to, it is an experience we can use when we want to understand the meaning of sonship. By considering the sonship of that to which we give birth, we can come to understand our own sonship. The parent, the teacher, the priest, the *senex* or spirit guide, the poet, the artist, the crafter are all included in the second or adult stage and form the class of parent, as do all who have disciples, heirs, descendants, successors, etc., all of which form the class of offspring—the members of which are always such that they can never be degraded into mere possessions of those who made them what they are. There is indeed no point in belonging to this class of offspring unless we are able eventually to "leave our father's house" and leave it in such a way that we don't become estranged from the mysterious and hidden source of our personality. When the time comes for the previous and the following generations to part, the progenitors or older generation should, if they have fulfilled their task properly, be able to find themselves amazed at the uniqueness of each individual they have generated. It is the proper state of human affairs for each young generation to surprise the older by its independence, and it is only proper for the older to admire the younger for this, since it is exactly what is necessary to teach the older generation what its own sonship means, how all sonship is nothing but our capacity for continual rebirth.

At this point I think we have reached a true understanding of what the old monk is supposed to proclaim when he becomes a true prophet: the proclamation that "God alone is true father, the true source of true life: he alone is our master and we are all brothers and sisters whatever the generation to which we belong."

If we can bring ourselves to understand life in this way, then each generation at each stage of human development will understand and respect each other, even though it will be only natural if this mutual understanding and respect has had the time to grow that much deeper on the part of the elders; deep enough, indeed, for it to be manifest to the juniors that their elders have spent that extra time in living the mystery of their own sonship. Here, then, is the ideal to which Benedict is leading us: the ability to hear the sound of water welling up at its source hidden beneath all the dead leaves that have been accumulating as we grew older; and not only the ability to hear that sound but the ability to tell our juniors how to listen to it, and to tell them in such a way that they are convinced that life comes from that listening.

Christ could see even further than the pious among the old pagan Romans whose ideal was found in the concept of justice, like the centurion in Luke who said at the cross "truly this was a just man." What Christ teaches is to seek perfection primarily in the filial relation between ourselves and God, a relation which in Christ's own case was unique, a relation that makes us, as sons and heirs, inseparable from God.

3. The Value of the Aged Monk to His Community

Let us start by thinking of someone who not only has reached a great age but who is a living example of the ideal painted by St. Benedict. Let us ask whether it is right for us to imagine that we shall find manifest in this old monk that perfection of sonship which we have been talking about.

At first we might think that it must be so, but on second thought we must surely realize that this would only belittle the long life of that ideal old monk which has been given him so that he might still continue striving for the perfection of charity, and so that the community might still continue helping him to perfect his *conversio*. Looked at in this way we see that there is something the community owes its aged members and something else that the community can expect to receive from them.

In the first place, it is important for the community to allow its aged members to remain part of the flow of its own life. In many cases the creative imagination of a monk no longer remains active in his old age. The wisdom of old age isn't a sort of encyclopedia in which everything is cut and dried and organized in its proper place. Wisdom is an art, and every artist needs to be part of a living society if he or she is to remain creative. It isn't enough for us to keep the aged up to date with the latest community news. We have to allow them to be part of the community's life and affairs, to provide them with an occupation, whether it is something that occupies their hands (and the monastery should find this less of a problem than an old people's home) or something to occupy their minds (and this will become a problem only for those monks who were never attracted to intellectual work). The community must also, and perhaps above all, provide its aged members with a chance for them to come to terms with their own past life (something of course that should never be encouraged in the case of monks who are obviously plagued by scruples). Our past should never be treated as something to escape from, for unless we can integrate our past into our present, we shall never understand the direction of our life and how it has been the path of our own individual progress toward God. To see what has unified our path, to see the whole of our life *as a whole,* to accept the whole of the reality we are, is to enter a state of peace. I shall return to this shortly, but for the moment I want to look at the community aspect of this ability to accept our past.

The community also has its past and it must, as a community, accept this. It must face up to the reality of its own history, something its aged members of course will be able to help it do, for they have a well-defined part to play in every historian's process of research and verification. The true history and the true spirituality of a community can be divorced only at the risk of falsifying both. One historian (fortunately not a Benedictine) has said how much he regrets the way his order has failed to implement the directive of Vatican II that urges institutions to return not only to the teaching of the gospel but to their own authentic origins. The past is what has led us to be what we are, and the suppression of history can do us no good. I don't mean we shouldn't enjoy our fairy stories and golden memories; what we mustn't do is let ourselves be satisfied by them—and the reason why is not unconnected with the reason why we urge novices to open their hearts.

When we urge upon a novice the need for opening the heart, we some-times make it sound all too easy and natural. In fact, far from being easy, it is quite impossible for anyone who hasn't understood what is meant by the freedom to which we referred. We can open our hearts only to the ex-tent that we have already achieved inner liberty, and monks can spend many long years before they achieve that. We may not have reached it even in extreme old age. The problem is, of course, like the chicken and the egg: this liberty can only be achieved by opening the heart; and yet, unlike the chicken and the egg, the solution is that the two things are done simul-taneously, but slowly and spread over a long time. The process is no differ-ent from that of our spiritual rebirth, the process of giving birth to a heart that is both free and open at the same time.

There is a spiritual art in helping the aged members of our community to achieve this perfect freedom of the perfectly open heart, and I do not mean giving them spiritual advice or anything else that might well have just the opposite effect. The point I want to emphasize isn't that, but rather how the question of helping the aged is closely related to the crisis of this present age, of the times in which we live, which are a turning point in human history, including the Church and our monasteries, a crisis that will show society whether monasteries have any value and if the daily details of our common life and behavior have any meaning.

Knowing how to speak of history and the past is like knowing how to speak to someone approaching death: both must be learned just as we have to learn how to speak about our own personal death. The way we do this depends not only on our faith but also on our temperament and even on the education we received as children. All of us share the same embarrass-ment when we have to tell anyone that we are soon to die; and if I can't offer you any original suggestions or advice, I can at least mention two re-cent deaths: those of Abbot Braso in 1978 and Abbot Simons of Kor-nelimünster in 1980. They were two monks universally admired, and each took leave of his brethren with great dignity and great tenderness, yet for neither was it easy to face death. From his own experience, Abbot Braso advised me never to tell people if their illness has been diagnosed as cancer—the last few weeks of Dom Berthold's life certainly seem to have been more peaceful. Each, however, was aware of the support they received from their community because even though the life of the community goes on, every community suffers death in itself when one of its members dies.

In its aged members, a community can find a reflection of itself. If the community is one that emphasizes the value of manual work, it will be nor-mal for its aged members to have some share in it; and in the same way any community with a true communal concern for the authenticity of its own life, whether past or present, will find that its aged members are not afraid to accept the totality of their own lives both past and present. The ease, however, with which the aged attain openness of heart is hardly ever the same in each community, and those in which it is easiest and most natural are those communities in which the members have developed the habit of offering each other help, a mutual help offered and received with absolute discretion and offered in a way that is the absolute antithesis of the polite small talk that reveals only too well that we are trying to disguise our indifference. Ideally, a community should learn how to show that its sorrow at the prospect of an imminent death is sincere, for then its old members will find the act of dying that much easier in the knowledge that it is a community act. After all, God himself celebrates the feast of All Saints at the death of each of us. This perhaps will have indicated what it is that a community can offer its old members.

If this is what a community gives the old—its own self, its own life— what do the aged members have to give the rest? One thing we have already mentioned is how the community can receive from its aged a fresh impulse to live by coming to understand, through them, the meaning of life. Another thing I would like to develop here is bound up with what is intended by the concept of "spiritual desire," with what is meant by the phrases "yearning in the spirit" or "longing for the spirit." When I was first asked about this topic in a quite unconnected letter, it didn't occur to me that I would need to speak about the sick, the aged, and the dying in my reply; and yet there is a connection. Extreme age is a time when many come to find that the body is something that keeps getting in their way, when it seems to be constantly obtruding as an obstacle and a hindrance. When we were young, and even not young, our body was never a burden we had to lug about; it was simply ourselves at a particular moment of development, but still perfectly adaptable because it was fully alive and able to carry on being the inseparable companion of mind. In old age the body comes more and more to predominate; so much so that the aged even start saying things like "I'm not myself any more" or "I'm not the person I used to be."

To expect medicine or hygiene to cure old age in the sense of restoring youth is absurd, but there is a sense in which we can use the word "cure": not *for* old age but *in* old age, since the word "cure" means making us fit to live the life that is proper to whatever age we have reached. We can't expect the doctor and infirmarian to treat us as if they were restoring a valuable piece of antique furniture to its pristine appearance. Their true aim, as it is the true aim of the cook and of the whole community, is to nourish, through the body, the inner treasure that Benedict calls "spiritual desire." Spirit is that heart or center of the mind, opaque and invisible to itself, but constituting all the difference there is between a living body and a corpse. It is that in us which is divine, that which makes the act of suicide wrong in anyone of sound mind, that which longs with spiritual longing for the

Spirit, that which is the great gift of the old monk to his community. It is the old who make it plain to us that spiritual longing has nothing to do with keeping healthy, achieving success, or copying others. It is something that can make beautiful even the ugliest face, even the body hideously disfigured by disease (and remember what Isaiah says about the Servant). It is that which gives the dying a desire to live in spite of any extreme to which their suffering can go. This is what we can learn if we visit the old members of our community.

If a whole lifetime has been spent measuring our earthly desires against our spiritual longing for Easter and finding out where they prove incompatible and how far they converge, then the spiritual desire of such a monk, purified by his great age, will have become a flame burning in him, an example of the paradox that it is the old who can speak better about desire than the young and lusty. When this is so, you have a monk who at the end of a long life has become what God wants him to have become: a son.

I myself have never been put in charge of either kitchen or infirmary, and it is only because I have spoken to others who have that I know how burdensome these offices can be and how much patience they call for. Monks need to confide the details of their health to the cook and the infirmarian, who thus come to know far better than any others in the monastery how long a road it is that we, their brothers, have to travel before divine grace makes our desire truly spiritual in old age. They are the ones, I suspect, who understand what was really meant by Lou Andreas Salomé, the friend of Rilke who wrote this line in a poem pointed out to me by a young monk only recently professed: "Having lived our youth, our youth lives on inside us." Happy the community where the youthfulness of the sons of God lives on in each, but especially in the old.

Denis Huerre, *Abbot-president*
Congregation of Subiaco
Sant' Ambrogio, Rome

Beauty and "Conversio"

Dear Brothers and Sisters of the Subiaco Congregation,

Wherever my journey leads, the beauty of this world meets me as I travel through it from monastery to monastery. Beauty is apparent to all of us, everyone can appreciate it, and we turn to it as a natural topic for small talk on any occasion. Recently, however, what has impressed me is how often, during private conversations, there have been references to the influence it can have on our lives. This turning of our mind to the beautiful, and Benedict's description of the monastic life as a spiritual art, are the two sides of what this letter is about: its topic will be the inner link between awareness of beauty and *conversio* of mind and heart. Beauty, after all, is nothing more than the visible manifestation of the invisible, and creation nothing less than the self-revelation of God.

Because creation includes not only the world or universe we live in but ourselves as living in it, our presence in it (as part of the whole) and its presence in us (through the mind and heart) is what makes *conversio* possible, and it is also what makes it possible for us to see how, in the *conversio* of each single human, the whole of creation is able to find its way back to our common source. Such being the case for everyone, its relevance to us as monks should be plain; yet, where the topic is so deep and I must confine it to a single letter, I shall have to limit myself to rather elementary remarks in the hope that by reading between the lines, the luminosity of our path in *conversio* will make itself evident in each of your monasteries.

As there are stages on this path that are common to all of us, I shall follow them in arranging this letter. It begins with wonder, to end (as the fragility of mere appearance fades) with the vision of that which is more imperturbable than the obvious: for beauty is precisely that which radiates as light or glory from the living truth.

1. Ecstasy, Beauty, and "Conversio"

The thing we express by words like wonder, marvel, astonishment, surprise, and "being left speechless" is a very ambiguous quality. We can find ourselves wondering why things are so awful or, just as easily, so wonderful. On the other hand, it would seem a little odd to speak of something that appalled us as being *ravishing*—though we can talk of a *raving* lunatic, even in England, where this word has lost more vitality than in France—we can still use it for describing parts of the liturgy for Christmas as being filled with a sense of *ravishment,* imbued, that is, with a feel of being transported into the mystery of incarnation. This sense of our encounter with the *mirabilia,* the marvels of God, is (for those who know them) exactly what the cribs of Africa, China, and Naples convey so well. This sense of wonder isn't confined to Christmas when what we celebrate is nothing other than the primeval blessing itself being renewed in the nativity. We encounter God's marvels again at Easter, when the renewal we celebrate is that of friendship between God and humanity. If each of these liturgies, in the cycle of the year, seems to follow the other so smoothly, the reason is that each, as a moment of history, is the complement of the other.

No human sin has ever been able to rescind that primeval blessing, not even what—in comparatively recent times and induced to do so by our own astonishment—we have chosen to label "original sin." From beginning to end, Scripture is nothing but a record of our human capacity for marvel. It expresses our wonder at this mysterious origin of all that exists in time and describes our wonder at its restoration with the coming of God's Anointed One. For this, the new creation, Scripture employs the very terms it uses for describing the first creation: the splendor of order emerging from chaos; the luminosity of the sun; the fixed unaltering pattern of the stars; the perfectness of a human body; the harmony of woman's union with man; the ideal beauty of God's house, built with that perfection of proportion which preserves it in the face of every peril; the majesty of the Word that is itself the very benediction it pronounces; and finally, those many things: bread, wine, oil, water, by which this same benediction enables itself to enter our mind through the very act of these things entering our body.

The marvels that can be described in those words are the identical realities that were established by the act of that primeval blessing; and not one single iota of all this is to be lost in the kingdom, when God himself, having entered our world to dwell among humans as human, and to manifest himself, in Christ, as the *light* and the *food* and the *house* of all, is himself received as gift and beauty and life. The beauty unfailingly manifested outwardly in all creation is God's own self-proclamation; to this, the only proper human response is ecstasy.

Love is born of wonder, and for each of us there must have been a share of that wonder in whatever it was that brought us in our youth to the monastery—whether in the youth of not yet being old or in the youth that grace perpetually renews. Since that share of wonder has led us away from home to come and share life with others, beauty has already played a part in the opening of our hearts and hands.

2. Work, Beauty, and "Conversio"

I have mentioned that *how* we are brought to open our hands and minds is itself a response to beauty; but even when the reverse is true, when our only response is to be overwhelmed, beauty still remains something which we encounter and which elicits our response; yet, though elicited, that response won't be passive. Novices learn quite soon that *conversio* isn't just a state of enjoyment; it demands inner effort, and the way it does that is much the same as the way in which beauty makes demands, both on those whose response is to create it and on those whose response is to contemplate it. Each of these ways of responding is an activity, and in each case this is so because outer beauty has entered and found it possible to continue its own proper activity from within. Beauty, as understood by an artist or a contemplative, has nothing to do with the decorative or the ornamental, with making things appear less boring or relieving our own boredom. Beauty and *conversio* are twin aspects of a single depth, and each is a revelation of the inmost essence of all that is. To penetrate that essence is the task that both artist and monk have set themselves, and neither can treat it as a pastime. There are moments and instances, of course, when everyone experiences beauty; but these are no more than fleeting signs of the Beautiful, of the supremely *ravishing*, by which we are inwardly *ravished;* and that alone is the beauty this letter is about.

To say all this, I have used that ambiguous word again: *ravish*, which is from *rapere*, to snatch, seize, steal, plunder, rob, or carry off. The fact is, when we are enraptured by the Ravishing, snatched away by the Beautiful, we are not being deprived of liberty. Freedom is the one essential human condition that alone makes possible our search for God. [TRANSLATOR'S NOTE: in English though not yet in French, we can resolve this ambiguity by using the new but now established word *ecstasy*.] What we are carried away from is the path we had been following, the inward path on which we entered as soon as the initial enchantments, insights, and ecstasies of our first *conversio* were over. Those are the obstacles that have to fade before we can start to practice our spiritual art as Benedictines.

What sort of task is it that Benedict expects the spiritual artist to undertake? Obviously, it can't be something that interferes with our regular occupations, such as listening to the Word of God or fulfilling our obligations to the recently deceased. The task is to enter the house of God, and our art is the way we do so by sharing the life, suffering, and glory of Christ. There the key word is *sharing*, a word that in the time of Benedict, though not in ours, indicated the *effort* we require to become like Christ through conformity of will. Now willing what Christ wills isn't a matter of trying to copy him. Doing what someone else would have done in our place isn't the same as just repeating what that person has already done. The distinction is between being actually like him and just pretending; between divinization and trying to appear holy; between being and imitating.

This applies to everything in creation, for there is all the difference between a thing being that which it appears to be and a thing which merely gives the appearance of being that way. To understand this is to understand the *nature* of created beauty and to understand *why* created beauty is so important for us. To see the obvious and visible beauty of something in creation is only a first step to seeing the invisible that it manifests, the first step that goes from using our eyes to see what is manifest to seeing with our mind that which is manifested; not unlike the more familiar step that all of you are making at this moment, which is from hearing words with the ear to understanding their meaning or truth by hearing these same words with your mind. The difference between the outer and inner of everything is the fundamental reason why we must never permit ourselves to despise the outer appearance of anything, however fleeting, since that is the only way we humans have of ultimately reaching the truth of anything that is always other than what it appears in its mere outer declaration. It is also the only way possible for *conversio* to work.

It is always and only the outer that can provoke our search for the inner. The outer can deceive us only if we allow ourselves to stop there. This is why, at every stage of our search, the moment of realizing our discontent with the outer doesn't become the moment we lose the joy that the outer has been giving us; it simply becomes the occasion for us to push on with our search. At such moments our minds are freed, the spell is broken, and we can escape; at such moments we recover the liberty we need to continue the search.

There is much we can learn from artists and craftspeople who talk about their work, whether that work is intellectual or manual, whether they are painters, composers, or scientists. Apart from special cases, their primary concern isn't with the creation of illusions, but with a search for truth, for ways of stating that truth and producing works that are true, authentic statements of being. Creative honesty and artistic sincerity is identical with the truth of that search which Benedict lays down as the essential condition for allowing us to enter the monastery.

Stage conventions for playing the part of a monk tend (unless the piece is anticlerical) to idealize him, and there are times when we expect our own brethren to behave like that in real life. On the other hand, the very reason we have given for never despising outer appearances means that we are not in a position of being able to reject the whole idea of "play acting." The fact is, we are all actors in the drama of life: tragedy and comedy are found inside the monastery as well as out. All conventions, monastic and theatrical, are concerned with appearance; and since the visible and manifest can never satisfy us in any shape or form, we ultimately have to turn to the invisible, to that truth which appears outwardly and is visibly manifested. This is the "turning" that actually constitutes *conversio,* the turning that actually defines our task, but it isn't something we can do once and for all, nor is it something we can indulge in just occasionally. It has to be continuous, for this is a task that is going to last us all our life. If we can see that, we can see what Benedict means when he speaks about spiritual art, and we can even begin to see how apt his choice of this label was.

There can't be many phrases that convey so immediately the importance of the *unknown* as what essentially characterizes every art and every search: the very thing that imparts to beauty and to *conversio* their inherent quality of mystery. Having called spiritual art a lifelong task, we mustn't run away with the idea that all it needs is determination. The artist has to be gifted, and the gift has to be accepted before it can be used.

Adveniat regnum tuum, thy kingdom come: this sense of coming, of what arrives, is exactly the sense of gift as something adventitious. Beauty is exactly that: something we encounter, something *there* that somehow presents *itself* to us, something that strikes us, something that has to be there before it catches our attention and sets us off on our long search by pointing to that which makes both beauty and *conversio* possible, by pointing to that of which beauty and *conversio* are signs. But what is it that is pointed to? Of what are beauty and *conversio* the signs?

3. Beauty, "Conversio," and Life as Encounter

The primary gift, anterior to receiving anything at all as gift, is *life* itself, and Francis of Assisi as its poet has wonderfully helped us to appreciate this in his Canticle of Creation. The beauty of the canticle's words may have charmed you already by their musicality and sheer simplicity; but what I want to speak about is the inner beauty of this poetic credo in which Francis affirms that every single thing in the whole of creation has the right to be addressed as brother or sister, since all alike are the works of the hands of God. Such an unbounded enlargement of the concept of kinship is a measure for us of just how totally Francis lived in the presence of God the Father, and how totally he identified with the least of anything created by the Father. The awareness of how his egotism had once imposed a rift between himself and all else, how it had split the seamlessness of creation, was the path by which he became the saint of reconciliation. As healer of every chasm created by ego, Francis unites in himself everything that is living, true, and beautiful.

What gives the Canticle of Creation its importance isn't the teaching on how to praise water, sun, earth, and air, but its view of all four elements seen as delighting in life; nor did they delight alone, for later, the final lines on death were added by Francis as the sign of what ultimately it is in creation that unifies all things as brothers and sisters: the fundamental *transience* that allows everything that exists to be the celebration of *Life;* and that has led me here to spell this word with a capital *L*.

The lifetime of Francis witnessed some of the finest analytical minds devoted to a study of the elements, but the route by which Francis approached them was his vision of beauty as so inseparable from the living God that everything is drawn into unity; by imbuing all things, including death, with beauty, which confers on them its own order and intelligibility. Seen in this light, it is creation's least desired aspect that is able, above all else, to make the Canticle all-embracing. It reveals how well Francis understood that only through the possibility of death does the living human mind provide creation with its possibility of transforming life into praise.

Francis' gift of a growing clarity meant that he was able no longer merely to *see* whatever encountered him, but was able to see *into* it, whether water, or the earth he loved to sleep on, or the trees that offered shelter to birds, whose freedom Francis now found himself able to share. Not many years after his death, that great Neapolitan Thomas Aquinas taught that what ennobles us more than anything is the sense of touch, for it is this which helps to sharpen our mental vision, a Thomistic doctrine we find verified in the life of Francis, whose mental vision pierced through everything tangible to God. How obvious it is that so many who think they understand him, who use his phrases and speak about Brother Sun, have not the least idea of that inner liberty which enabled Francis to speak as he did. In place of his vision that could penetrate to its ultimate truth, their view of the sun is limited to treating it as an object that mind can grasp and whose existence can cause delight. Such, alas, is the ignorance of the sunworshiper. What Francis realized was that however much beauty makes its appeal to the five senses, the beautiful is such only because it is able to penetrate through them into our mind. Here it is that we can see how intimate are the links between beauty and *conversio*. Beauty is unable to bypass the senses (and this is the reason we can never afford to despise sensual delight), but the function of our senses is to enable beauty to penetrate within, to become that to which the heart of our mind can give assent.

From the second century onward, beginning with Origen, an entire literature grew up devoted to the "spiritual senses," which is only a way to help us speak about how we are penetrated by beauty; about what it is to encounter beauty; about how it is that that which beauty engages must be the whole of what we are, the totality that comprises the senses, memory, and imagination, as well as spiritual insight; about how it is that through this action of beauty all these aspects of being human are able to intercommunicate and integrate themselves into ordered harmony.

To say that the function of beauty is to produce this harmony of all that each of us is mustn't be understood as meaning that all we have to do is sit back and let it happen. On the contrary, this is a task presented to us as humans, and thus it isn't anything other than the lifelong task we have identified as *conversio*. Approaching it in this way, we see the absurdity of imagining that we are supposed to be dead to the senses. If there can be no manual labor unless the mind sets the hands to work, the same is true about our monastic guard of the senses. What would be the point of having neighbors if a cessation of our sense consciousness was the only aim we had in common? It would mean begrudging that very life, the totality of which Francis never ceased praising.

The aim of Francis was to live in unbounded communion with all that exists. His poem about this has only two stanzas, so we can quote it in full to demonstrate the beauty with which he gets the second to balance the first:

> *I love the sun, I love the stars, I love Clare and the sisters*
> *I love the human heart and everything beautiful*
> *O Lord, forgive me*
> *it is you alone that I am meant to love*
>
> *But the Lord was smiling when he said in reply:*
> *I love the sun, I love the stars, I love Clare and the sisters*
> *I love the human heart and everything beautiful*
> *O Francis, what can I forgive?*
> *I love the same things as you*

Only his love of being alive gave Francis this possibility of encountering such beauty in so few lines—and how well his poem shows us the absolute indissolubility of beauty and *conversio*.

4. Beauty and "Conversio" as Our Encounter with Love

Let us turn for a while from Umbria to Old Castile, from the sun to fire and John of the Cross who, about 350 years after Francis had sung the praise of creation, wrote his Spiritual Canticle as a commentary on the Song of Songs. The Christian tradition of commenting on this began quite early in the Church and, during the lifetime of Francis, a silence that Benedictine monks had kept on this book of Scripture was being broken by writers like William of St. Thierry, whose commentary seems to have been the inspiration for that of John of the Cross. Like William, John set himself to compose a meditation on the praises of beauty that God and humanity never tire of addressing to each other.

Written for two human voices to sing in a mutual admiration society, there would be nothing essentially unbalanced in such a dialogue. What makes the Song of Songs incomparable in itself is that neither of the singers can be compared to the other: one is creator and the other creation. The only thing they might appear to have in common and which makes the singing possible, is the love that they have for each other; but human love and divine love can't be compared any more than God and humanity. This is why a remark that William makes is so perceptive: as the singing alternates, each song makes it possible for us to study not the singer, but the object of the singer's praise. On the one hand is the divine bridegroom, the supreme good that alone can be our ultimate joy; on the other hand, there is that which God himself can see, and this is nothing other than his own goodness reflected in us to the precise degree that we find joy in him.

Here William has discovered the essential key to understanding how the song is possible at all, the key to understanding how it is possible for the self-images of the divine imagemaker to grow in union with him through growing in likeness to him; how beauty contains the beautiful, and goodness contains the good (Cant 1:8). What William echoes here is an insight achieved by the noblest minds of pagan antiquity: the unbreakable bond between beauty and goodness in their undifferentiable unity. What John of the Cross adds to this insight is that beauty is solely and wholly divine, and the human is beautiful only insofar as it is receptive of the divine. Yet when, and insofar as, the divine beauty is received, the duo between God and humanity becomes possible and the singing of the Song of Songs lasts as long as do the gifts we receive from God.

This is an appropriate place to quote the important lines from stanza 35, but they need to be read slowly because the involuted balance of their intricate thought. [TRANSLATOR'S NOTE: Allison Peers in his note on these very lines indicates this as the reason all manuscripts vary in their reading of the passage, which isn't part of the poem but part of John's own exposition and commentary on a single line of the poem. The translation offered will, it is hoped, be slim enough to convey the sense in a single reading.]:

Rubric
the Bride says

Poem
Let us go and see ourselves in your beauty

Commentary
This is the adoption of the sons of God by which we, as members of the Mystical Body, can say with Christ: All that is mine is yours
All that is yours is mine

Explanation
For me to see you in your beauty
is for you to see me in your beauty

since
then it will be that in your beauty
you will see yourself in me
and I shall see myself in you

but
for me to be myself in you
    so that
    my beauty is your beauty
    and your beauty is my beauty

means
that in your beauty
    I must be you
    and you must be me

for
only then
    will your own beauty
    already be mine

It is in this passage that the Doctor of Love, John of the Cross, shows how love and beauty are one. Our goal in *conversio* is that having become (through love of God) like God who is love, we become love like God, so that what he loves in us is his own beauty that we have come to share.

Is John still talking about people on *earth?* Am I keeping to my subject, which is *created* beauty? In each case, yes, because when (as in the life of Benedict) our human mind is enlarged by the infinite, we don't cease to be creatures. Only by remaining what it is can creation be illumined by the light of this love and, once illumined, it is this illumination of creation that is its re-creation and makes it the new creation. William of St. Thierry (a little before the passage already quoted) says that knowing and loving are the two eyes we need for understanding: one for understanding the human according to the rules of science, the other for understanding the divine according to the rules of wisdom. Without love, knowledge is dead; without knowledge, love is blind. A little further on, and taking up the principle laid down by Benedict that there cannot be any such thing as a place that isn't suitable for our encounter with God, William becomes even more explicit about the worldliness of the setting and says: this exchange of praise between God and humanity takes place on earth, in our ordinary everyday life, at the very moment we find ourselves being overworked or having difficulties in prayer. William hasn't just kept his feet on earth; he has kept them firmly on our own familiar ground of the monastic life.

John, of course (if we can turn back to him), had to keep his feet on less familiar ground inside a prison of the Inquisition. That it is earthly beauty of which he speaks becomes explicit in the concluding lines of his canticle that he devotes to the five gifts from the bridegroom. Here the important thing isn't the particular sensuous images chosen—the grove, the song of Philomel, nightfall, the heavy scent of summer air, and so on—but the reason why he needs this sensual imagery at all. Having traveled through the canticle, our final station is that which we reach when God himself breathes in us, when it is not only creatures that sing of God but God himself that is singing through them, and in such a way that it is this very song that is actually creating all the creatures we see and hear; for every creature is his song, and every one is created by this god-song as a gift for his Bride. This is the stage when we no longer know God only through knowing his creatures, for now we know these creatures through our knowledge of God.

This teaching of William and John is nothing other than the teaching of Benedict, though the way they put it may be a help for you to understand the lifelong task of our spiritual art. The very heart of our mind is being purified from within by the Holy Spirit. It is beauty itself that is within us, and through its presence we learn the language in which the text of creation is written; and having learned how to read, we find we can read that text unceasingly no matter where we are: in choir, workshop, garden, or on our travels.

5. The Narrow Door: Christ's Death as the Revelation of God's Beauty

We haven't ever been taught that we are saved by this world's beauty, but only by the death and resurrection of Jesus. The function of created beauty is to awaken us to what it is and so to draw us away from our self-centered egotism; and thus, though it is true that Christ alone is our Saviour, it is by his beauty and by that alone that he saves us. To speak, however, of this beauty of Christ dying on the cross to rise from the dead, we need to choose our words carefully so that they don't confuse us, because this is an area where, as von Balthasar warns us, we can easily be misled. This warning doesn't come in his main work on the aesthetic aspects of faith and revelation, but in his detailed study of the nineteenth-century romantic theologians, whose tendency to mix up beauty and the romantic means that—for all their talk about a theology of beauty—they couldn't set their sights higher than making theology sound beautiful.

The concept of Jesus as glory, as beauty radiating like light in every direction to infinity, implies not only that this beauty which is Jesus must fill the whole material world visible to our eyes, but also the human, immaterial mind that is invisible to itself. We, as created, should be filled with that beauty which is Christ, the creator of life and Lord of all that is within creation. For us, however, who need salvation, life as we live it is distorted, so that often we are more like lamps gone out than lights shining out. To share our nature at this inmost source of human experience where in consequence of sin we experience death, Jesus freely accepted to die.

It is here, in this acceptance, this elimination of self ("not my will but your will") that we find the outer expression of his inmost beauty. For him as much as for us, this death to self is what constitutes the Narrow Door, so narrow indeed that only this selflessness of acceptance is small enough to pass through. The beauty that remains on the cross is concentrated at this inmost and smallest point; nothing of Christ's beauty has faded except the wealth of its outer evidence that was accumulating all through his life on earth: his ability to speak as no one else had ever spoken; the power of attracting disciples with a gaze; the power to sleep in spite of the storm, to join the banquet at Cana, to be silent before his judges. All this had been only the outer evidence of his real, inmost beauty remaining with him on the cross, the beauty of that same inner assent to God in which Jesus perfected the assimilation in himself of all that is human in creation. In him, the human world discovers the perfection of that path to beauty, which is nothing other than this very assent willingly given in life at the moment of death.

Life has never been short of its problems and traumas, yet we don't spend the whole of it simply anticipating what the next disaster will be and rehearsing our reaction to it. There were many years that von Balthasar spent analyzing the works of playwrights over several centuries in order to catalogue all the varieties of human drama for his book *La Dramatique divine*, in which he shows how even the minor frictions between characters can be illumined by the role of beauty and love in the drama enacted by Jesus. Von Balthasar is only the latest in a long line of Catholic thinkers who have pondered the human dramas of everyday life as having a role to play in God's dramatic creation. A function of love and beauty in our life is to show there isn't any audience: we are all on stage.

The fact that we are all, even at this moment, acting on stage, doesn't mean that we are helplessly caught in some gigantic trap. To every character in his play, the goodies and baddies alike, God has given the gift of being free, so that even the victims in the worst of all possible scenarios can choose to be in touch, at their inmost, with the perfection of beauty and love. We can all identify with the terrorist, converted on his cross at the side of Jesus, because every human is created for the sake of the beauty reserved for the prodigal son.

Think of the beauty of Simone Weil, who found in the poverty of the poorest her vocation to perfect love, or the beauty of Maximilian Kolbe. Every monastery has its share of these: their lives may have seemed very ordinary until, right at the end, we see them become a living assent to the living God. When absolutely nothing whatever had led us to expect this sudden flash of beauty, it really does become something unforgettable.

6. Practical Considerations

All our monasteries know examples of this sudden beauty, since that of which it is a sign transcends every difference of life-style and nationality. Beauty is such that it cannot be renounced even by monks who renounce everything, for beauty is inseparable from Christ. Bernard of Clairvaux never felt called upon to give up trying for perfection either in prose or in architecture; it never occurred to Benedictines and Carthusians that in the art of copying manuscripts we could ever aim at anything less than making perfect copies that were beautiful to look at. On the day of their profession, Carthusians used to be presented with the tools of a copyist, and the workshops in which these tools were used can hardly be described as hovels. Tourists have every right to be astonished when they visit ancient abbeys turned into famous museums, and the same desire for our faith to be expressed in fine craftsmanship is found exhibited in the modest buildings of our own more recent monasteries. Beauty, by its nature, is inseparable from truth, and the friend of God is instinctively the friend of humanity and the friend of nature.

This desire for beauty in a monastery is perfectly natural even when attempted, as it sometimes is, with such appallingly bad taste. Generally speaking, the taste exhibited in our own monasteries can best be described as mixed. Short of having good taste imposed on us, this will surely be inevitable and it does at least have this advantage: it allows a certain enlargement in the field of our asceticism. There can't be many communities that haven't experienced the heated debate of a chapter discussing some proposal for a new building, a new organ, or a new fresco. Obviously we have to put up with the inevitable and make the best of it, but making the best of it doesn't mean doing without a little mutual education. This might at least clear up the popular misconceptions common to people with no training in art, but far more importantly, it might help to overcome the sheer ignorance that seems to prevail in monasteries as to what exactly it is that artists are saying in their work.

No one of course will expect us to reach a balanced judgment overnight about anything, and least of all about art. We can be expected, however, to try to improve things gradually, which is the way, after all, we have to work on our own *conversio*. Every aspect of our lives has to cooperate on this slow path; we can't take short-cuts and get simple do-it-yourself kits for becoming Christ-like. Like Jesus himself, we have to respect what people are, and that must include all the things that make them what they are, and we must do this for the sole purpose of helping each other in the search, which is the one thing necessary. There just isn't any other way for the reign of God to become on earth what it is in heaven. Nobody has the answer to everything, and all our monasteries need monks whose teachings can educate in that area of life—spirit and mind—which is the area in which beauty and truth are studied. Nor, in this respect, can monasteries afford to neglect the importance of books on modern art. This isn't a matter of having them on open shelves where they can satisfy idle curiosity, but of finding a way for their meaning to be explained to the community.

The fundamental requirement in all our houses is, in effect, to broaden our mind in the whole field of aesthetics, in our appreciation of beauty in its double aspect that we mentioned earlier: in its creation and in its contemplation.

a. Creation

We all have gifts and we all have work to do. Through appreciating and developing these gifts, our work can become a creative reflection of beauty. Every job we do, including our intellectual studies and the liturgy, is an area where the beauty we seek can become more and more actual, providing only that one is open to, alive to, this possibility. That means, of course, being equally aware that every job and task is an area where beauty can be destroyed or suppressed.

b. Contemplation

Above all, we must meditate on the inconceivability, the inexpressibility, of God; on our inability ever to grasp what God is. This is the one and only meditation that can guide our attempts to express the inexpressible. In this respect we can learn much from the history of iconoclasm, both before and after Islam. A theology of incarnation can't avoid reconsidering the theological reasons that led to an absence from synagogue, early Church, and mosque of any representation of God in human form. [TRANSLATOR'S NOTE: the human form as such isn't absent, e.g., from the synagogue of Dura Europos; and when the Prophet destroyed the idols of the Ka'bah, he expressly preserved the icon of Christ and Our Lady, which remained in place till the Meccan fire—long after the death of Muhammed—destroyed the Ka'bah. Ecumenically, the stance of Jew, Catholic, and Muslim alike is that, par excellence, the image of God in human form is the human being in worship.]

Paintings of the crucifixion are known from before the end of the persecution and, life being stronger than suffering, the canons of classical humanism eventually prevailed. No artist can ever be satisfied by existing representations of God made human, and no attempt at representing Jesus can ever be taken as final. Artists will always seek something further to portray, and we can never reach a point where their search to give figurative expression to the Word incarnate is finally concluded.

We are taught to see Christ in everyone who turns up. The Benedictine artist is able, therefore, to take as his model for Christ the very first person he meets at random, and before such an icon we should have no difficulty in meditating. It may not be an image of someone beautiful according to our human standards, but monks are meant to see deeper than that, to see the truth declared by this icon as that which can be seen only by the light of faith, the beauty that our knowledge of God has led us to see in every part of creation.

As in every aspect of *conversio,* our own personal encounter with beauty, whenever it presents itself to us, will always entail the deepening of silence. At Sant' Ambrogio a sense of this silence is what prevails on an evening we spend listening to recordings of the monastic office that monasteries sometimes make for profit, sometimes for their archives. Just the other evening it was Prinknash and Stanbrook. What these tapes convey is the beauty of our relationship with God; for in listening to that, as St. Augustine noticed, we achieve in an instant the realization of how time and eternity are united.

Denis Huerre, *Abbot-president*
Congregation of Subiaco
Sant' Ambrogio, Rome

Desire and Conversion

My Dear Brothers and Sisters,

This letter represents my efforts at clarifying an area to which my attention was directed three years ago. An abbot was discussing what criteria we should use when judging a vocation, not only at the time of first profession but at the time it begins to dawn on someone that he might be called to the monastic life. Soon after that a nun brought up the same problem, but from a different point of view: how a vocation is perfected in habitual abandonment of self to God. One was concerned about the starting point, the other about the goal, but both were clearly talking about that single thing which makes it possible for a vocation to start and for it to reach its perfection. Now that single thing is desire, and desire is as important in making life truly human as it is in making life truly monastic.

When I tried, however, to send a reply to that abbot and nun and began writing about desire, I discovered just how difficult a topic it is and this, in fact, is my third attempt. It may not be better than the two previous attempts, but it will at least no longer start from the assumption that I can give them an answer. This present letter has been written instead as a contribution to a subject which is not only important and difficult, but which is becoming the object of much serious reflecion in our monasteries. What it comes down to is how desire and conversion relate to each other.

The aim of the first part of this letter will be to formulate a hypothesis after looking at two questions, the first of which is whether and how far we should assume that everyone in vows is liable to some weakness in his or her resolve to keep them. Try to remember the liturgy of your own profession and its triumphant celebration of your desire for God, the search for whom is the whole point of taking vows in front of witnesses who, as such, now acquire the right to be called brother and sister, since it is their search for God that we are to share. The whole beauty of this liturgy stems from the fact that it celebrates the covenant, the marriage of God to humanity. And now look back at the reality of your profession as a whole as Benedict does in one striking detail that shows how aware he was of what all ancient traditions, including the biblical ones, anticipate about pacts and treaties.

Never is it thought enough merely to express one's resolve and intention through symbolic gestures like reading the promises aloud, signing the text, and depositing it on the altar. A second stage follows that is equally essential: the superior takes the document from the altar and locks it up to be used in evidence against you. Trust and mistrust are inseparable, though the second half takes place so rapidly that its single gesture of collecting the incriminating document is particularly eloquent. The possibility of any monk breaking his vows cannot be ruled out; this single gesture is the expression of a profound anxiety.

Psychologists and sociologists describe exactly the same kind of anxiety being exhibited in ceremonial details of engagements, marriages, and every sort of agreement and bond that people make between themselves. The anxiety, in fact, is inherent in every human decision, however freely that decision is made; and the reason for being anxious is that we can never tell what the future will bring, we can never rule out the possibility that something unforeseen will crop up. A verbal promise should always be enough to bind us, but society demands something written and signed, and even adds further symbolic acts and gestures. In the example of marriage, for instance, we have wedding rings, wedding dresses, wedding gifts, the wedding breakfast, and so on. Now all this is intended to exorcise the demon of anxiety, the thing that worries the witnesses as well as the parties concerned. This demon of anxiety is driven off even more effectively when the ceremony is couched in the actual form of an exorcism with threats, both veiled and open, against the unfaithful partner; threats familiar to Benedictines from the Rule. Every promise has this weakness inherent in it, however much and however sincerely we intend it to be perpetual. At every profession, both the community and the new member are taking a risk, and this is the reason the whole community must bind itself by obligation to help the new member.

The second question is about the search for God, that is, about our reply when asked "What do you seek?" What I am concerned with here is how this search is initiated and who initiates it. The first question we looked at was about the promises taken in public because of the degree to which public interest is always implicated in the private affairs of its members. Here we are going deeper than that, into something very much more private. What has prompted us to make such a promise in public? There are off days when we all ask ourselves "Ad quid venisti?" What on earth, ultimately, was it that we *did* want?

Benedict's repetition of the question only confirms what we said about his fear that something could always crop up and undermine the desire we affirmed at our profession. To ensure that our desire remains authentic and effective, there has to be some constant habitual appeal to the conscience and personal liberty of the professed monk. This is provided in the Rule by the community, which has as one of its functions the obligation of perpetually calling to us to recall our promise. Failing this, it would not be a gospel community, for it is by their own desire for God that our brothers and sisters keep alive our own desire for him; and this is done, of course, tacitly rather than explicitly.

Now that we have seen how it is that all vows have an inherent weakness and that a community is there to help keep us alive to that question "what do you seek?", it is possible for me to formulate my hypothesis, which I do as follows. There would seem to be two main reasons that make desire, of its very nature, mysterious, something obscure and unobvious. Either reason will be enough to make it *obvious* that desire has to be *unobvious,* but since each does so from a different approach, they do not depend on each other, and so the two reasons are not symmetrical. Let us call these two reasons "the unconscious" and "the unknown." The unconscious (or subconscious) is part of us and produces effects on our conscious life, yet, being out of sight, we can't study it directly, even though it is a most intimate part of the person *who* desires. *What* the person desires, however, is unknown, since, necessarily, it is that which we want to know. The unknown provokes our desire and attracts it, the subconscious provokes our anxieties. Attraction and anxiety coexist in desire.

Information about our subconscious is hard to obtain and amounts to little more than scraps that appear to have neither rhyme nor reason. In spite of their being disparate and illogical, we have, however, been able to work out something of the logic behind them. We know, for instance, that the subconscious is continuously there, and being aware that it is a continuum, we can say that our subconscious could be described as an area where desire is nothing but mere desire; not desire for this or that, but simply pure desire as such and nothing more. There is nothing we can do to control it, and the fact that we cannot rationalize it seems crazy and irrational. The net result of all the work done by analysts on the subconscious is sufficient, in spite of contradictory findings, to suggest that our best approach is to stop trying to influence the subconscious and instead simply allow it to influence us and our conscious desires. These desires of which we are fully conscious are the reasons we give ourselves for living, and all we can say is that they have their roots in the subconscious and that this, being below the level of consciousness, will always remain mysterious, unobvious, and obscure. The *obvious* thing is that some link does exist between the subconscious and what we are conscious of. The *infuriating* thing is that we can never see this link. I rather tend to feel that this in itself is probably enough to account for anxiety. The more we try to penetrate into our subconscious, the more we approach a cave into which we cannot enter, and yet we are perfectly aware that this is the place from which all our desires originate.

Our desires come to us, at the surface, from this cave that we can never enter, but they are directed away from the cave toward something in the opposite direction that is equally mysterious. Their source is the subconscious that we *can't* know and their object is that which we don't *yet* know. However certain we are that we already know God through Christ and that our faith is a certitude and our knowledge of this certitude is manifestly real knowledge, yet it is true that the Most High will always be nameable only as the Unnameable and will always be known only as the Unknowable. Whatever view we take about the so-called natural desire for God, it will always seem extraordinary that Adam or anyone should be like God, that Abraham or anyone should be the friend of God, that anyone, like ourselves who are baptized, should be children of God; yet so we are and fully aware that God who is Being isn't "a being" such that we could ever grasp him, and fully aware that we, as "beings" in the process of becoming, are not ever going to advance to some spot where we reach the stage of a totally perfect likeness to God beyond which there can be no further advance. Union with God can *never be static* but—as Benedict says—consists of desire, of our search for God.

On the one hand, we are conscious of the unconscious, and this worries us and makes us anxious, while on the other hand, we know that God is unknowable, and this fascinates us and draws us on, makes our desire unquenchable, urging us perpetually forward. This remains true when this urge is unbalanced and turns into frenzy, and it remains even truer when this urge is so perfectly balanced that it turns into peace. The monk is one who desires and who desires to always go on desiring.

So far we have had a look at those two questions (the ease of forgetting our search for God, and the value of having others to remind us tacitly of it by their own search for God); and we have also had a look at my hypothesis that desire is necessarily mysterious because its *source* is known to be unknowable and its *object* is known to be unknowable. Here I can conclude this preliminary part of the letter by adding the following:

Everybody who is involved in providing witness to a profession (and that means the community in general, but the abbot, novice master, and spiritual director in particular—the saints whose relics are present and the whole communion of saints including angels are also witnesses!) will need the discretion that is able to remind the individual perpetually of his or her freedom to continue that search along a path which, since it leads to God, is *unique* to each of us, but which, being *universal* and common to all human beings, must depend on the way all human knowledge is limited by these two unknowables, since they are the reason that however much humanly we can explain about a vocation, we can never actually explain the vocation itself.

At this point I must exercise a little of that discretion myself, as I want to follow this hypothesis with three reflections addressing desire in us, desire in Christ, and (that puzzling term in the rule) spiritual concupiscence:

1. Desire and Ourselves

Since monks and nuns are human beings, we share the sort of desire that is common to human nature, including that of Christ. What is more (and here we are unlike Christ), we all share the experience of sin. The path we follow after profession is still the same path of desire common to all human beings, and our monastic *conversio*, for all that makes it a *monastic* conformity to Christ, will still follow the patterns of change common to all human beings, which will either lead us to maturity or lead us to the need for a new conversion.

Now try, if you can, to think of two connected things: on the one hand the history of each of us, and on the other hand, the history of the entire human race (or the entire universe) up to and including ourselves existing today. The distinction here between those two histories and the way they relate to each other is probably quite enough by itself to explain how most of our desires get brought to the surface. The question that should interest any monk is what happens to these desires once they reach the surface and we become aware of them? Let us look first at the path these desires actually take, and then at the way we can train them to take the right path.

a. The Path of Desire

Let us begin with a conclusion that psychologists would seem to have established quite firmly. Desire is never a matter of sudden impulse. It grows slowly and is always in a state of becoming. Since we can't say anything at all about it when it is still in the stage of the subconscious (before we are aware of it), we can only start discussing desire from the point when it begins to gradually emerge, however vaguely, into our awareness. The stages of its slow development have, in general, been very clearly mapped. First, we all start off as self-centered babies and then slowly change when, in infancy, we become aware that there are things which are not ourselves. Only when we start relating ourselves to what isn't ourselves, can we begin to live for the sake of others. This is the path of desire leading from selfishness to altruism. But then, having reached out from self to other, the path can begin to lead back in the journey of self-discovery. On this path which is our life, however, there are two notorious pitfalls that some people fail to avoid. One is the trap of becoming self-absorbed and the other is the trap of allowing oneself to get absorbed into an impersonal Other.

This slowness is true for everybody, but it has a special relevance for those who have a vocation to the monastic life, because it is by this slow path and, indeed, right at the center of what it is that we are, that each of us evolves into what it is that a human should be. Monastic life being lifelong, it must always be geared to a slow pace. Always be suspicious about a sudden conversion because, though they hardly ever happen outside literature and folklore, this is the reason Benedict protracts the period of waiting before profession. Modern psychiatrists and Benedict have different approaches to what monastic desire is; in spite of this, we can offer the following remarks under the three headings we have already mentioned: self-centeredness, the loss of this, living for others.

SELF-CENTEREDNESS

This should never count against candidate, who want to enter the monastery, since all of us have to be aware of ourselves and sufficiently aware to be aware of our own liberty. For some this will mean being aware of exactly what they want and why they want it, and even of what their chances are of getting it. The danger signs are when this concern with self is a clear case either of scruples or of severe withdrawal to the point of isolation from reality. Psychiatrists and Benedict agree on this. The self-centeredness that concerns a monk, however, is what Benedict identifies by the traditional and technical term "self-will," what we variously term the "false (or unreal) ego," the "false personality," with that which grows when everyone and everything is referred to it alone. Now this growth is something that started in all of us as a perfectly normal phenomenon at the stage of babyhood. It only becomes seriously harmful if it persists after childhood and we resist the effort of educating us out of the blind alley of egocentricity. Where this infantile attitude persists in a grown-up, it produces adults who behave childishly and tyrannically; but in all of us it remains the root of all our worst aspects: our lust for power and the craving we have to dominate others by owning them and controlling them. It is the root of our tendency to oppose everything that doesn't fall in with our own desires. This is what self-will means and, as it hardens, it imprisons us like a nut in a shell, a shell that needs to be broken if we are to achieve our freedom as humans.

ESCAPE FROM EGOTISM

We don't escape from this hardening shell by the desire to have no desire at all or by the desire for others to impose their will on us. To want things in this way is simply to feed our egocentricity. No false ego will disappear by trying to negate itself. We have to be clear about the difference between desire and want. When people know someone is planning to enter a conventual community, they often accuse him or her of trying to escape the harsh realities of life, but a novice who shows signs of being motivated by a need for a social setting in which he or she feels secure should never be thought ready for profession. The difference between desire and want is that desire is always for the unknown and is easily stifled when all our wants are supplied.

Take the parable of the two sons: the model for monks isn't the elder brother whose stability in the family home showed him to be such a filial son of the father. It is the younger prodigal son who (as Benedict says in the Prologue to the Rule) returns home through desire, or, to be more precise, who is driven to return home by his need to eat, but he discovers that his selfish need (eros) is transformed when he sees his father coming to meet him as God comes to meet us.

ALTRUISM

Quite a number of writers these days seem to be impressed by the way Benedict manages to define what it is that we have to be if we are going to become truly human. In the Rule, of course, this is only worked out insofar as it applies to monks who are cenobites, professed solitaries living in common. Every time I mention that this is what monks are, it seems to provoke an unexpected interest; but solitude and communion, far from being inherently opposed to each other, are inherently linked, and so much so that human reality demands both, since both are essential if we are ever going to explain how the path of desire gets safely from its source to its goal, providing it avoids the two extremes of isolation and fusion that we mentioned above.

Before we turn from the path of desire to how we train desires to take the right path, let us note this new point we have managed to establish for testing our candidates. Are they sociable enough or are they too sociable? Have they that minimum that is necessary to try living in a community based on the communion which grows from the solitude of each member and which strengthens that solitude as it grows?

b. Training on the Path of Desire

This growth of a communion that strengthens the solitude of each member is the very thing that takes so long and forces the path to be slow. It explains why a monk isn't simply what one is in consequence of entering the monastery, but only what one becomes after entering. The slowness of the path is the rate at which the monastic life is lived. I want now to devote the rest of this section to training (which concludes what I have to say about desire in created beings), to three crises in life rather than to all the stages we have to pass through in living it. These three critical moments of life are three experiences that have to be used in the training of desire: the experience of need, of loss, and of gift.

THE NEED TO NEED

Need, want, lack, craving, demanding, requiring, envy, as well as a lot of other similar words, can all be used to illustrate the fact that we are not and never can become self-sufficient. We *are,* but only by way of *becoming;* we *are,* but only insofar as we *depend.* Infants quickly come to realize their dependence on others. Adults need to realize their dependence at the fundamental level of totality. There is, of course, the sort of totality people dream about: achieving total happiness, reaching a total understanding of the universe, creating a total harmony in all society, in one's local community (like some monasteries and some states achieving unanimous votes). The immediate need for each of us isn't to indulge in this dream world but to establish harmony between the interior components of our own totality, of that wholeness we are, which is body and mind composed without any mutual antagonism in need of each other.

When the Rule offers us a way of being perpetually aware of what we lack, it does so to protect the freedom and desire of each member of the community. Any candidate for profession must face not only their own insufficiency but that of the community. By accepting this, our desire becomes what we live, becomes our life, and we make progress and move forward into joy. Either we advance through this inner awareness of want or we perish through the thought that our every want has been supplied. Anxiousness and aggressiveness are the marks of the rich.

THE NEED FOR LOSS

One obvious example of this is the mourning of others when they die, but it isn't so much the death of others that we need to experience as their distance. We need this distance to live a more interior personal life. Partings can be painful, and it is this sort of pain that is a necessary condition if our perpetual becoming is to make us free enough to accept what can only come as gift.

THE NEED FOR GIFT

What use is any gift if we have to lose our life to get it? But there is in the gospel another loss of life, not the one that makes it useless to gain the whole world, but that loss of life by which life itself is gained. This is the death that allows us to be reborn as truly human, which we are only when we deepen our interior solitude at that point where one is perpetually open to the perpetual gift of what lies perpetually ahead. This gift, which is given only as the awareness of our need, is the very gift that allows us to discover that there is more joy in giving than in receiving. A dangerous sign for any monk is to lose this joy, but joy in this sense isn't the same as mere enjoyment and pleasure. It isn't easy to explain the difference briefly, and I can't stop here to go into the question; but if the function of the brethren is to *remind* us of our desire to search for God and so to *purify* our desire, we need to realize that we can't help them in that way until we understand the distinction between the two sorts of joy and understand the place of each in the monastic life.

The first topic that we have been considering up until now has been "desire and ourselves," that is, "desire and the created human being," including "desire and the candidate seeking admission" who, once admitted, will spend his or her whole life discovering what it means to be a created human being, a being in the process of becoming. Our createdness is something sacred that we have in common with all human beings, and no one can be faithful to the thought of Benedict by evading or minimizing the importance of becoming fully human through the monastic life of desire. As far as the candidate is concerned, we are not expected to make a decision merely on the basis of what it means to become a human. The next two sections will deal with further criteria; but nothing in those following sections will be valid if we fail to see their roots in this section or forget that it is only here they can be firmly rooted. On this point Benedict is particularly precise: the ladder is constructed out of body and mind joined together by our deeds that constitute the rungs by which we make progress in *this* life. Jacob's angelic dream ladder isn't ethereal for Benedict either. It is how God is present to us in this life, how God encounters us, how God comes to search for us, how God reveals to us his desire, how he does this through Jesus Christ. So from desire and ourselves we can turn to desire and Christ.

2. Desire and Christ

Jesus of Nazareth was fully human; yet, as he himself tells us, he was without sin. That being so, how can one even begin to talk about his desire? In the first place, no one could be human without the desire to live; in the second place, desire isn't the same as sin. Being sinless, the desire of Christ is unique and it is this that makes all the difference between this new section and the previous one.

The paradox of Christ's desire is more precise than his ability to desire without sin. We can imagine this fairly easily. What is much more difficult for us to imagine is that his desire was totally devoid of self-seeking or self-cherishing: *pro eis sanctifico meipsum.* This is why the paradox effects our salvation. Being devoid of a false ego, he can tell the holy women (tell us) not to weep for him on his way to death, but to weep for ourselves. We desire so many things, but the desire of Jesus was unique and unified and never dissipated like ours into a multiplicity of contradictory objects. At the level of psyche, the level where psychiatrists work, this absence of plurality in desire would present a problem, one that even Christian psychiatrists admit they could not solve. This singleness of desire that makes Christ unique means that no one else has ever fit the definition of a monk, of a *monozōos, monotropos,* or *monachos,* as Jesus does by virtue of the fact that he is the *monogenes,* the only begotten of the Father. The substance of Christ's human awareness is formed by the singleness of mind made possible by his sonship. Jesus was able to have doubts, to ask questions, to learn things gradually, and he did so; but all the while he was able to maintain the singleness of his desire and to do so at least from the time of his bar mitzvah in the temple as an adolescent ("this is my Father's house") until the time of his death ("Father, as you will"). Far from falling into the trap of self-will, of self-cherishing, his desire remained pure; not the pure desire of the subconscious, but the pure desire of the fully conscious; not pure because it lacked any specific object, but pure because it desired purely for that one thing which all desire is intended to be for.

On one side stand monks like ourselves with multiple desires; on the other is the uniqueness of Christ and his unique desire. Plainly, what is needed is that all our diverging desires should converge at the one point to which his is directed. But is this possible? Is this focusing of the totality of our desires just another case of dreaming about some unattainable totality? Benedict gives a very clear answer: we are not meant to stand here gazing up in admiration after Christ. We are to participate in the uniqueness of his unique desire. This is what the whole Prologue is about. In all the Gospels there is only one desire that Jesus had, which is actually named for us: his desire to eat the Passover with his *disciples*. Consequently, the one desire that we, his disciples, should have, is to share his passion and resurrection. Here then, and to begin with, we can see how his desire and our desire can become symmetrical and converge. This is precisely what Benedict proposes to his monks. Each of us is to progress from multiplicity to singleness in body, mind, and heart-of-mind. Though it isn't natural to us for our multiple desires to be recollected through singlemindedness, it becomes natural through our participation in the unique desire of Christ.

Much of what I have been saying merits deeper thought; what I have said, for instance, about suffering and death; and this seems to be a good place to look at that again. Since we can't be suggesting an actual death of body or mind, what exactly *is* this "participation"? To concentrate on the word "death" would seem to mean that we could participate by the death of all our desires, which is absurd because that wouldn't unify their multiplicity. What we need to concentrate on isn't the word "death," but the double phrase "death-and-resurrection." The two sides of this phrase are inseparably linked, as we discovered when we became Christians, in the very act of passing through the baptismal waters. The baptized live yet don't live, for (as Paul says) another lives in them.

By refusing to limit our desire to this or that within creation, by not confining our desire to the corporeal and temporal, we aim at the unity of Christ, and we aim at it by living it for the whole of our lives. Stoics understood what *conversio* meant, but we take that meaning to a deeper level: the conversion of our desire is its conversion into the desire of another who descended to our level precisely for this, since what we are to participate in is the uniqueness of his *human* desire. It isn't that our desire becomes his desire just because we desire it. Desire won't change desire, though many authors, including Christian ones, use the phrase. Our desire to participate in the desire of another can be fulfilled only if the other desires it, and then, at *his* desire; the desire that actually participates in his desire remains *my* desire, and yet now no longer self-centered. To understand participation is to understand the nature of escaping from the trap of self-centeredness. Christ reveals to us not only the Father but what it is to be a human. He reveals me to myself.

3. Spiritual Concupiscence

Having considered what is the difference between desire in ourselves and desire in Christ, we are in a position to see how natural it is that Benedict should combine *spirit* and *concupiscence* into this phrase that at first sight seems so unusual. The two are no more incompatible than *heaven* and *earth*, which Christ combines in the injunction to do on earth the will of the Father as it is done in heaven, by which he gives us to understand that "earth" isn't merely matter as opposed to spirit. The course of history has, at times, witnessed Christians, including Benedictines, making spiritual freedom the pretext for carnal license, but I should think Benedict in the sixth century was even clearer than most of us about the nature of self-cherishing and egotistical desire. The Rule has two passages that demonstrate this, but Benedict saw no reason to harp on the point and contents himself with summing up the right attitude in what he says about loving chastity in preferring Christ and his unique desire.

Benedict's approach is, quite simply, no other than the approach that is made by the Holy Spirit. The Rule demonstrates this three times over: If the name of the Father is ceaselessly on our lips, that is the work of the Holy Spirit; if our ceaseless desire for Easter brings us to the Son, that is the work of the Holy Spirit. The third demonstration is the way the work of the Holy Spirit is seen in the combination of all three Trinitarian passages on the purification of heart that end the Prologue, only to be taken up again in chapters 7 and 73.

The meeting of God's living desire with human desire is *how* the Holy Spirit comes to us, and this coming is never delayed, never deferred to a time after we have encountered Christ. To encounter one is always to encounter the other, and this rules out all possibility of illusory desire, that dream of some future kingdom of God on earth, some historical period in the future when everything is totally transformed and spiritualized and made perfect. It is because the kingdom is so different from this fantasy that I want to end by saying a few things about sublimation and sexuality.

a. Sublimation

To sublimate anything isn't to idealize it. Ideal and idol have rather more in common than their etymology and, in fact, all the idols we are constantly making for ourselves tend to be idealizations, some more removed from reality than others. We can apply this to what I said above about totality. If something captures our interest and we are led to imagine or hope that all our desires concerning it might be fulfilled, then that is idolatry. If we find it impossible to desire more than there actually is, more than the whole of everything, then that is idolatry, and it spells death to any desire for the infinite. Humans, after all, can desire the infinite (though we can't have an infinite desire for it) but to have that desire means being aware that what we desire transcends every possible totality, transcends both the All and the One.

On the other hand, sublimation has nothing to do with having an obsessive, one-track mind. One way of explaining this might be the following: think about the energy that we spend. We spend it in every effort we make, whether the effort is physical, emotional, or intellectual. When we make an effort, we direct our energy at a specific target, we spend it on getting what we want. But if we direct our energy beyond that target, beyond any target, beyond all targets and toward nothing but the infinite, then that is what sublimation is and that is how it works. The farther beyond the target our energy is directed, the more it is sublimated, and so it is most perfectly sublimated when directed at that which transcends everything.

From this we can see it is the transcendent, and that alone, which unifies the energy dissipated in our multiple desires. Since this is surely the most constructive view to take of monastic celibacy, we can turn now to sexuality, which, as I said, was to be the final point I wanted to speak about in this letter.

b. Sexuality

A letter on the "conversion of desire" can't omit the question of sex—perhaps I should have brought it in earlier. The first thing to get clear is that celibacy isn't a way of escaping our sexuality but a way of expressing it. This means we must understand it better than we have done, perhaps, in the past. The second thing to get clear is that sexuality won't be understood if we can't understand its spiritual aspect, and this is no more than part of what we were saying with regard to Christ's teaching about the will of the Father being done "on earth as in heaven."

[TRANSLATOR's NOTE: The distinction in French between sacred and holy doesn't quite exist in English, where even to talk of God's "saintliness" would sound odd. As a result, what the President says here about the difference between the sacred and the holy, and about sex being holy but not sacred, can't be easily translated into the terms he uses. The following may help to convey his thought which, at this point, also becomes rather cryptic.]

Sexuality isn't an object but part of what a person is: objects can be blessed, but only persons can be canonized because only persons are free. Human life is that living freedom which alone has the possibility of *growing* in holiness. This is what makes self-transcendence, the escape from our false ego, possible in the continuum of our life. By transcending all those specific targets that were mentioned before—including those that attract our sexuality and so are in question here, all those multifarious appearances to which our senses are geared, to which our sexuality is geared—desire itself is unified, and all those targets are integrated into our life and into the living worship we offer in spirit and in truth. Any target of a specific desire (and not necessarily one of those attracting our sexuality) may prove more difficult to transcend; hence the many spiritual combats of the monastic life, but hence, too, the possibility of that perpetual advance in ecstasy.

4. Conclusion

With these remarks I conclude my letter, though they don't conclude my study of conversion and desire. Nevertheless, there are two points of some importance that seem to emerge from what I have said: (1) We don't give up freedom by taking vows. It is freedom of conscience that makes our vows possible, and what we vow is to avoid the loss of that freedom by maintaining it as our one desire. Without that freedom, any desire I have would not be *my* desire. It wouldn't even be God's desire. It would be something so impersonal as to be insidiously dangerous; (2) solitude isn't isolation. Anyone who turns the solitude of a cenobite into an isolation faces a danger that is even more insidious, since this will lead to the rebirth of self-will, which, above all, is the trap that a monk has to avoid. If now I finally conclude by saying that growth is what I desire most for your community, you will know it isn't growth in numbers but an ever-growing intensity of desire in each of your members.

Denis Huerre, *Abbot-president*
Congregation of Subiaco
Sant' Ambrogio, Rome

Pentecost 1987

Liturgy and "Conversio"

Dear Brothers and Sisters of the Subiaco Congregation,

To continue our reflections on *conversio,* this letter considers it in relation to the liturgy. Should we think of liturgy as the setting in which *conversio* can take place, or is it better to think of it as simply one aspect of *conversio?* In other words, does *conversio* begin or end with liturgy, or both? Is there anything in our vow of *conversio* that suggests we should not become liturgical scholars, but rather performers of liturgy? After all, the Rule doesn't mention the word "liturgy," so why should it have any special meaning for a Benedictine?

I have chosen this topic in response to an article by John Gale in *Studio Monastica* 1985 (27:1): "The Divine Office: Aid and Hindrance to Penthos." If you read it, you will probably feel uneasy, and were we all to accept its conclusions, we would have to change the way we celebrate our monastic liturgy, since we would find that it was more a hindrance to *compunctio cordis* than a help. It rather takes the line of what one monk is supposed to have told his abbot, that nowadays it's hard to see any connection between the monastic life as we live it and what Benedict laid down in the Rule.

Someone who was both a great spiritual master and a liturgical expert might be able to give you an answer to all the problems that this raises. I certainly can't, and all I intend to do in this letter is to offer my reflections on how these problems affect two of the important aspects of our life: our interior *conversio* of the heart and the amount of time we spend in choir. Anyone reading this letter might be able to approach these questions better than I can, but the point from which I start is going to be the obvious one of the Rule.

1. "Conversio" and Liturgy as the Way We Celebrate Christ the Conqueror

In the Rule, as Père de Vogüé has pointed out, the candidate is someone who has stopped hesitating between the Two Ways: he has chosen *the* way, the Way of Christ. The mere fact of choosing the path isn't, of course, going to make the path any shorter. All it can do is to help him travel with a lighter heart. On the other hand, he knows as well as we all do that the monastic path isn't a cul-de-sac. It has a goal, and the goal is in sight, and the path goes right up to that goal. Here we see the importance of Christ being shown to us in the New Testament as Victor or Conqueror, because in him we already share in his victory. This is why the Rule, though it is perfectly clear that any monk who sets out on this path retains his ability to sin, and may actually even commit sins, makes it equally clear that sin, having been conquered by Christ, can be avoided by preferring him to all things. This is one of the points on which, as Dom de Vogüé has also pointed out, the Rule of the Master is less clear than Benedict. The Ladder is our life in *this* world, whereas according to the Master, we have to wait for the next life before we reach the twelfth step.

At this point it may help to remind ourselves that the baptized have entered both the death and the resurrection of Christ. The early Church found this particularly important: at baptism we are renewed, and sin should no longer be something normal. During the 1983 synod, which studied reconciliation and penance, Père Jean-Noël Alatti, the Jesuit who is professor both in Paris and in Rome, said that while the Old Testament talks a lot about confession of sin but not so much about reconciliation, the New Testament says little about confessing sin but (and especially in Paul) a great deal about reconciliation. Christians were the conquerors who had overcome; they were called "the saints." John says in his first letter (3:9), "Whoever is born of God sins no more, because the seed remains within him."

John and Paul are at one in their theology of God reconciling the world and renewing its friendship with him at the very moment when our human hostility toward him put Jesus to death. Through his gift to us of *conversio* and reconciliation, God awakens in us the ceaseless liturgy of joyful praise described in the Apocalypse. What produces our decision is the decision of God that preceded it, so that *conversio* and liturgy are only the two essential aspects of triumph.

Nevertheless, though we are conquerors with Christ, we are also the conquered, vanquished through our weakness. When the New Testament was written, the majority of sinners were the unbaptized, and yet even then the baptized committed sins. The early Church experienced the same sort of shock as the new state of Israel in 1972, when it faced the incredible fact that in spite of having been founded on pure and lofty principles, the moral and social disorders of the old nations of Europe could still reassert themselves. How was the early Church to deal with sinners? Especially public sinners? What sort of efficacy could one attribute to baptism? Was there a case to be made for rebaptism? Should sinners be assigned a special status within the Church? But then to what part of the Church could they be said to belong?

These questions all helped the Church to clarify its ideas about excommunication and to work out a practical penitential discipline with workable regulations for the sacrament of penance. These were not things that could be decided all at once; they began a process that didn't just go on for centuries but is still going on and one that will always be going on. The two-fold mystery of God who forgives and of our human response to that forgiveness is the mystery of how we, as conquerors, can still be the conquered. This is expressed in the liturgy through alternating chants of victory won through Christ the Victor, chants of compunction when we become aware of our weakness, of the dust that settles on the white garments we wore at our baptism.

Yet the way the liturgy alternates these two strands allows it to put the overall emphasis on celebrating the victory of Christ. If at times the element of compunction becomes dominant, it always ends by becoming subdued. The liturgy has its own rhythm, like the alternation between breathing out and breathing in, between pride in its outer proclamation of Christ and its inner descent to the *humilitas* and peace that comes when the self is pierced and wounded—when our ego is "pricked" ("com-punctio") like a bubble. Every jubilation in the liturgy should be enough to remind us of our nothingness, of how true for each of us is the message of the gospel, Ezekiel, and Jeremiah about sinners.

The liturgy is celebrated in different ways in all our monasteries, and we all have different reactions to the way it is celebrated. Since it would be invidious to single out instances, let me give two pairs of examples from the past that don't have any connection with our congregation. In 1147 Pope Eugenius III was present in the abbey church of Sant' Denis for the blessing of Abbot Suger's great cross, which he had encrusted with precious stones gathered from every district of the kingdom. Two other abbots were present and all three were eventually beatified: Peter the Venerable of Cluny, deeply impressed, had perfectly understood that he had been invited by Suger to celebrate a triumph of the Cross in which nothing offered God could be too excellent. The other abbot was Bernard of Clairvaux, feeling thoroughly miserable and convinced that what Suger had invited him to was nothing so much as a triumph for the monks of Sant' Denis. What *he* looked forward to was the next day when they all went to consecrate the new altar in the church of the nuns of Sant' Pierre on Montmartre.

The second example is from the same year. We have a description of liturgical splendor in the celebration at Athens on the second of February, when someone found himself impressed by the sight of the patriarch and his clergy, by the chant and incense rising mingled to heaven, and by how the clear sound of thurible chains and bells echoed the clarity of Greek sunlight. Later, in Jerusalem, the Ethiopians celebrated an equally unforgettable liturgy in their poverty-stricken chapel that, owing to the lack of space in the anastasis and in order to be as near the Holy Sepulchre as possible, is situated up in the rafters.

What these monks of east and west can teach us about *conversio* and liturgy is that triumph and compunction are equally real, and that we must learn how to treat them as equally real, and to do this by seeing that they are inseparable from each other. All liturgical rites have their own rubrics, all are held in equal honour, and it isn't the rite that is important but the way we participate in the liturgy itself; because there is nothing that takes place in any liturgy more important than what takes place in our heart and mind as we celebrate it and understand why it is that we are present at the celebration and what it is that we are celebrating. Whenever we let liturgy disguise our need for *conversio* instead of showing it to us, we alter our values and reduce our standards to those of theatrical excellence, to a level that isn't able to express the meeting of the Savior with his Church and hasn't got the power of putting each member of the Church in touch with the Savior.

2. "Conversio" and "Liturgia": The "Memoria" of Our Creator

The phrase *opus dei* has two meanings; only the second one refers to the liturgical prayer of our monasteries, to the work that *we* do. The primary meaning refers to what God does, to his operation in us; and yet both its meanings point in the same direction, which is the direction we are to take. To understand how this direction relates to *conversio* and liturgy, we need to understand why Benedict prefers to speak about our *return* to God rather than about our *journey* to God. The most obvious reason is that Benedict speaks about God in accordance with the Creed. The one God in whom we believe is equally both creator and triune. As in the hospitality of Abraham, it is the three persons of the Holy Trinity that we entertain daily, and it is the operation of the Holy Trinity in a monastery that makes it Trinitarian, as was mentioned in a previous letter. In this letter I want to see how we can balance this double view of God as the creator of all and the creator of each.

Here I must avoid becoming lyrical (something Benedict was never accused of) while I explain how I like to associate God the creator with the moment a monk gets up and goes to join his community in thanking the creator for the justice of all his decrees. Is it fanciful to imagine that these early hours relive, when we pass from sleep to conversation with God, the first appearance of human beings in creation? Isn't sleep a sort of nothingness from which we pass to the fullness of faith? God is there calling my name and I don't have to hide at the sound of his voice. Isn't the whole symbolism of nocturns our passage from night to the dawn of Easter, to the dawn of the first day of the week, to the dawn of the first day of creation, to the dawn of Christ's return at the end of time? I find the whole sweep of time becoming coherent through these associations.

These days, theologians have had to apply their minds particularly to the mystery of God the creator, and the greatest help they are offering us is on the journey of our return to God in the spirit of Benedict. The Christ we prefer to all things is the Creative Word, and what the Word reveals is that human sinfulness isn't something that God's primordial intention had failed to take into account. The deeds we do can't produce any alteration in God. What they can alter is ourselves. We are able to change, and if we belittle ourselves by the harm *we* do to ouselves or to others, then equally we are able to grow; but this is the way we alter ourselves because of what *God* does.

The mere fact of being created, of having been brought into existence and kept there, is enough to give a direction to our life and so to impose on human beings an obligation to follow that direction in the life we live. I gave a little example of this when speaking about the monk who grasps the true reality of daily life by thanking God for it as soon as he wakes up. It is having this direction that makes it possible to talk about our royal priesthood. The dignity of human, of Christian, life isn't simply that of kings, but of kings who are also priests.

Each day is a new beginning, each day we wake up able, like a new Adam, to thank God the creator and prepared to be his co-worker. When Paul talks about us as God's co-workers he makes use of the Greek word *synergism*, which means exactly the same as the Latin word "co-operation," and co-operation means, in the first place, *work*—this includes the work of prayer. But work means doing a job and (as far as we are concerned) doing a human job; but according to the way we do them, all the tasks we have to complete are themselves converted and transfigured into the work of God.

The following anecdote may not mean much to those of you who are not electronics engineers, like one novice in a monastery I visited who explained the technical meaning of the word *synergism* in English. [TRANSLATOR'S NOTE: Perhaps I could preface this with a quotation from the new supplement to the *Oxford English Dictionary:* "synergism: the combined activity of two substances when this is greater than the sum of the effects of each when present alone." Synergism isn't just addition; it's where the results are greater than the sum of the parts.]

In electronics, *synergism* means that some effect is greater than the sum total of the energy put in by different sources. The point of the comparison (which may not be very close) is that it might help us to think of ourselves as plugged into Christ, though not in the hope of producing a result greater than if we each acted separately, but so that any help we offer others may produce in them an effect that isn't only greater than what we would expect, but different from anything that we might have imagined.

This is how the *Lumen Christi* that we celebrate at Easter is renewed every night in the monastery: through the power of the Spirit of Christ, we are able to begin each day as new creations. [TRANSLATOR'S NOTE: English isn't logical enough for the words "rise" and "rise again," "turn" and "re-turn" to help us see *conversio* and liturgy as not only related to each other but as inseparable. What we can see as fairly obvious is that if they are inseparable, then we should never allow ourselves to think that there must be some sort of conflict between the solitaries and the cenobites. Benedict makes provision for each of them, and it would be completely false to restrict compunction of heart to the hermitage and liturgical celebration to the monastery.]

There were, of course, the celebrated cases where certain solitaries went beyond what is essential to *penthos* or compunction of heart and invented all sorts of spectacular penances against which Benedict warns us in the chapter on Lenten observance. Writers who talk about Benedict as though he reduced the amount of mortification obviously don't realize that the *vita communis* that he substitutes is something much more difficult, and it is this extra burden of the common life which shows that Benedict and the great heroes of the desert were animated by a single spirit. They were all obviously equally delighted at having thought up just the way to outwit the devil. That is another hint for us at how *conversio* and liturgy unite in celebrating Christ the Victor.

If *conversio* and liturgy are not to be separated from each other, neither must be separated from the state of things as they were when they were still fresh from the hands of God. What I am trying to say is that before there was ever need for human work to be integrated into the path of our redemption, work was a sign of our human dignity, and it remains that, even though sin has added another element to it. Life becomes monastic when it integrates work and rest, hospitality and food, reading and study. Since each of these elements is an opportunity for *conversio,* each of them is an occasion for thanking God, and so we see the whole of monastic life as an integration of *conversio* and liturgy.

Nowhere does the Rule suggest that God is more present inside the oratory than outside it. All that is special about the oratory is that it is the place where a monk can hope to become more aware of God's presence everywhere. If prayer is ceaseless, there is never a time when it isn't at the interface where past and future touch, where the division comes between what has just been completed and what is just about to be done. Surely this is what the various forms of that medieval motto are trying to convey, whether *ora et labora* or *laborare est orare.*

A cenobite, of course, has one special temptation, which is to forget—while making his own contribution to the work—the need to take a real interest in the work that the others are doing. One function of the liturgy is to teach and remind us that all outer technical correctness, whether in the liturgy itself or in anything else, is hollow and empty if our mind has failed to cultivate communal charity. Benedict is indicating this when he points out that pardon must come before praise. It is the forgiver who is forgiven and, as such, the monk is able to live for others and for God and so to live for himself as well. In a community that lives, works, and prays together, each member will have come to his own understanding of what the word "together" means.

3. "Conversio" and Liturgy: Waiting in Joyful Hope

Christ has come, Christ is yet to come—but how can anyone actually live in the perpetual expectation of meeting him? In itself, love is divine and doesn't depend on time, but, essentially, time is the actual living of a human life. All expectation involves waiting, and this waiting is what gives it importance both to our own inner time and to time as the measure of history. The happiness for which we live isn't only a future reality, but the very same happiness that has already begun to grow in our life. What makes it grow is our work and the way we accomplish the task set us as human beings. What it grows toward is that sort of eternity into which time can grow.

Something that can help us to become more aware of life as waiting for what we look forward to is the sheer monotony of living according to the Rule. The "joyful hope" of our Christian expectation is nothing different from what life itself is when we live it in the certitude of faith. And that, of course, is a very different thing from trying to fix our will on a goal that attracts us and then forcing ourselves to try to reach it as quickly as possible. To be able to wait patiently is an exercise in *humilitas* as well as a display of courage. We can even find ouselves getting impatient when waiting for someone who actually turns up on time.

Monastic life isn't only monotonous, it is also repetitive: we go on and on, saying the same things and doing the same things over and over again— and there is nothing that helps our stability to grow more than this, as we become more and more aware that the goal to which we stretch forward is that very thing we have discovered in the heart of our mind—what we most desire. This interior awareness of our own interiority that makes us aware of God, aware of what is *other* than ourselves, is what eliminates egotism and is what makes us aware of the need for words and deeds to come from the heart of what we are. This is an inner, and so a more real, link between *conversio* and liturgy, between life as joyful hope and life as our response to him who is to come.

We all have the perpetual problem of how to stop our words and deeds from becoming stale, mechanical, and lifeless. Most of our monasteries since Vatican II have made the attempt to inject a sense of life and reality into the liturgy. This hasn't simply meant a lot of changes in the liturgical books; it has meant a change of mentality, a real attempt to understand and explain our biblical and patristic texts; and even more than that, an attempt to ensure that the texts are read and sung meaningfully, to ensure that the meaning is actually listened to and understood. This has made us all the more aware that the very nature of what we celebrate and of what we proclaim is beyond the understanding of even the deepest mind. Liturgy can't be made easy and reduced to the obvious and ordinary. Least of all can it be made easy for the listener who tries to assimilate and understand what is being proclaimed aloud by all the texts, as well as what is being silently proclaimed by the ritual ceremony.

This is why it was found necessary to add moments of actual silence as a third element to the words and the gestures of the liturgy. If there are cases where these make their appearance as if they were a hitch in the ceremony, they are not fulfilling their purpose, which is to allow us an opportunity for mental *conversio,* without which there isn't any praise and thanksgiving for the words and gestures to proclaim. Each monastery has its own way of incorporating these silences, and my feeling is that were they to be excluded, the liturgy would tend to become a mere formality, something that has to be gotten through before we get on with the next thing.

Nevertheless, there are moments in the liturgy, apart from the silences, which do seem to be conducive to *conversio.* In the first place, there are the psalms themselves, because the ceaseless repetition of the Psalter is essential for the monk if he is going to assimilate it and make the words part of himself. And we need to do this because of the extent to which these words have become impregnated with so much of what we mean by humanity and Christianity. I am not concerned here with the best way to distribute these poems or how to organize their singing or the best music to sing them to—there are people who understand all that far better than I do. What I am concerned about is that we should aim in choir at being like that desert father who said that when he recited the psalms, the words came out as if he had composed them himself. They should say exactly what we want to say to the One that we prefer before all things.

Another moment in the liturgy especially suited to *conversio* of mind is the sacrament of reconciliation. Here everyone must follow the rhythm that is best suited to him, and in general these days, people have recourse to it less frequently than they did in the recent past. Being a time when we acknowledge the truth about ourselves, the sacrament is able to offer the monk something far wider than what is suggested by the words of absolution, something that in fact covers the whole field of compunction. A piece of advice given by Vatican II is that if we really want to live a sacrament, we can only do so in the context of listening to the Word of God. We can, for instance, read a passage of Scripture before confession, or we could go through it with the priest. As well as helping us to turn our mind to God, it should help us to recall among our failings and omissions some of the really deep personal things that are so easy to forget. One experiment I might mention here that monasteries have tried in all sorts of different ways is that of occasionally having a community preparation for confession so that afterwards, when one goes to receive absolution privately, it becomes more obvious to us that this is something we are receiving from the whole Church, since it is only in the Church that one is reconciled with God and with our brothers and sisters.

A third liturgical moment favorable to *conversio* is the sacrament of the sick when, as so often nowadays, the whole community is gathered round the bed and we can become more aware of the whole Church praying with us for someone whose illness we can see for ourselves. It isn't just that the moment itself is simple and solemn but that we can't meet for any liturgy afterwards without remembering it. These really are occasions when an entire community can seem to share a common sense of waiting in joyful hope.

Lastly, we can mention the Mass itself as a fourth liturgical moment, the one that is specifically focused on interior *conversio;* and yet, partly owing to the very fact of the Mass being the fullness of sacrificial liturgy, and partly because I attend it so often, it seems to be the most difficult liturgy in which we can participate fruitfully. I doubt if any one single monastery has yet managed to find the right balance between Eucharist and Office. This may be due to all sorts of things and not just the way Mass is being celebrated, though one source of the problem is certainly the double cursus of readings and another is the simple fact that in no area of monastic life is the difference so great between the way it is now and the way it was in the days of Benedict. This isn't a thing I can go into here, since the letter is concerned only with the relation between liturgy and *conversio,* so perhaps I can end the letter simply by saying the following. To go to communion, to receive the Body and Blood of our Lord, is, in the first place, nothing less than to allow oneself to be transformed, converted into him. His life becomes my life. In the second place, it is our entry into communion with all members of his Mystical Body. Eucharistic communion and fraternal communion are two sides of what communion is. During Mass, the decision to communicate must be the free decision of each individual. No one should feel pressured into it through fear of being different, and this is particularly important in monasteries where there is only the one Eucharistic celebration each day. It also raises the question of how far it is necessary these days to relax the ancient liturgical fast.

Conversio and thanksgiving express what is special about monastic community, because they are what make a community monastic, and they in particular are what make it a community of compassion to the point that our guests can become aware of this quality in the monastery. No monastery can ever be a place of sinlessness, but every monastery should be a place of forgiveness. The aim of its liturgy can never be the applause of an appreciative audience, but neither can it be considered a monastic prerogative. The liturgy in the monastery is still the liturgy of the whole Church, the liturgy of the whole human race as *the* pilgrim progressing to our common goal. As Augustine says: If a pilgrim sings, he sings because of his conversion.

Denis Huerre, *Abbot-president*
Congregation of Subiaco
Sant' Ambrogio, Rome

Epiphany 1988

"Conversio": The Abbot and the Monk

My Dear Brothers and Sisters,

These letters on *conversio* have made me face a number of difficult questions that I think it would have been wrong to avoid. Now I find myself facing one that is doubly difficult. I could take a theological approach and simply ignore the human aspect; or I can take a psychological approach, and the very thing I want to talk about—the relationship between a monk's *conversio* and his abbot—becomes reduced to the techniques that promote good relationships in a community, as if it were a machine needing constant maintainance. Obviously, I must try to bring out the connection between these two levels: one, the reality of the supernatural; the other, the real conditions of our life here below on earth where the *conversio* of a monk takes place.

I doubt if a Christian could find any way of discussing *conversio* that didn't come around to seeing it as the direct result of Christmas, of time being entered by the timeless Word who is from all eternity. Through *conversio* a human involves God in our world, in the whole universe or cosmos. What is made possible only by the existence of time and duration is what makes it possible for God to evaluate what the monk's personal liberty has made of a life that was given on a particular day but given to last forever.

That is the context in which I want to look at our problem, and it really is a difficult one. What possible role can an abbot have in the long slow *conversio* of a monk? What sort of role can we possibly assign to a person who, though he isn't God, is known by God's name of father or abbot? After all, he only received that name through being elected by us, and our votes can't change him in any substantial way. We have to look at a role given by our votes to someone that we expect to carry it out irrespective of whether he is loved or feared, capable or incompetent; a role that he is going to fulfill either as a useful servant or as a useless one.

The first part of this letter will echo and sometimes quote the conversations that I have had with those of you who are abbots and abbesses; the second part will be addressed to those among you who are not yet and who may never be abbots and abbesses. The first part will contain my reflections on the role of abbot or abbess and the second part will explain how the abbot or abbess, being one of the tools provided for our *conversio*, can, if properly used, lead us into the unexpectedness of perfect liberty.

Monks and nuns are already the children of God, though only insofar as we are in the process of becoming his children. The liberty of the children of God isn't just the air we breathe. It is also the air we are learning to breathe. Abbots and abbesses may not be the only witnesses to that liberty, but their role makes it possible for them to efface themselves, and it is that which makes them privileged witnesses.

PART I: WHAT CAN ABBOTS DO TO HELP IN THE "CONVERSIO" OF MONKS?

Conversio is a work that requires a workman and a workshop. The workshop can be nowhere else than in the heart of the monk, at the heart of his mind, and the workman has to be someone with access to that heart, who can get inside the workshop. No abbot can do that—only the monk himself. All the abbot can do is teach his monk to descend into that heart and warn him of the solitude that awaits there and persuade him that this loneliness is what he must not try to escape from. The work itself consists of the following: the discovery of one's own innerness; learning what gifts we have been given; estimating our own possibilities; purifying the desire that first started us on that journey; seeing that this descent into our own nothingness is literally endless, learning from experience how to avoid the pain of having taken a wrong turn when we realize that our descent into the endless *mysterium* of our innerness has become only a quest for some inner self and that the proper name for what we have been doing is self-seeking.

An authentic descent (which is to the nothingness we are, not to the something we are, however small) will mean that our inner mind is enlarged through becoming aware of our own *humilitas* or nothingness, and of how different that is from the small-mindedness called pusillanimity. How can one avoid these wrong turns? Spiritual guides who help others on the way of Christ must always be careful when speaking of recollection, silence, and interiority, to show how the awareness of being present to ourselves leads to the awareness of being present to God who makes us his dwelling. God is closer to us than we can ever be to ourselves, but in such a hidden way that language lacks any words that could convey this to others. All that an abbot's words can do is to point to it: only the monk is able to become aware of that presence in himself. That the monk will do this is what the abbot hopes and prays. To experience that presence is to become aware of the *otherness* of that workman whose work it is to bring about our *conversio;*

not doing it instead of us but by making his otherness the root from which our work grows, the spring from which our work flows. He works *with* us not *instead* of us, and yet that work is truly the work of the Holy Spirit, whose role as the sanctifier, as the one who makes us holy from within, is indicated with great clarity and on three separate occasions by St. Benedict.

That said, we can turn to the question of the abbot. Now the abbot is neither a substitute for the monk nor a substitute for the Holy Spirit. He has his own place in the work at our "heart" or center. It isn't the place of a father; God alone is our father. People sometimes enter a monastery in the hope of finding a substitute for the father or mother they have left behind, but there are no replacements for parents. However appalling they may have been, they are the best we are ever going to have. Other men and women can't take their place.

Many monasteries have brothers and sisters who have never known warmth at home and who have never had a home. The community has to compensate for that and be an environment in which affection can grow and mature. But eventually all of us have to progress beyond the stage of home life. We need it to be human, but only as a transient stage that is going to help us progress to the stage of separation, which is so plainly seen in the life of Jesus, and which he tells us is essential in the life of a disciple. But don't be misled into thinking that "separation" means wiping out all our memories of the home stage. It doesn't even mean being indifferent to them. Retaining and cherishing our memories, we enter a new way of being, a new way of loving, and only this newness separates the two stages. If we had to stop loving and being loved, we might as well stop living.

I have said enough to show why I think it unfortunate to talk about the role of an abbot or abbess in terms of family life. Even to call the monastery a "family" is highly ambiguous. Thank God I have been allowed to have the experience of both family and monastic life. I can see the similarities between them but also the profound differences. Monks shouldn't be encouraged to rediscover their childhood happiness, and abbots shouldn't be encouraged to treat the community as his family. Many abbots, however, are only too happy to give up the role of *paterfamilias* because they think their proper role is to take the place of Christ. That immediately transfers the abbot to a higher order of reality that can only be seen with the eye of faith. It is in fact a view that I used to share, and I don't have any regrets at having tried to carry it out. Yet, these days I am coming more and more to realize the ambiguities of saying "the abbot holds the place of Christ"; not because anyone might think it meant abbots had the *power* of Christ. The truth of what John XXIII once said is too obvious: "I'm not Christ, I'm only the pope." Christ "stands at the door and knocks," but abbots can't even get near the door. Can they do more than pray from afar that the heart of their brothers will open when Christ is heard knocking?

I can illustrate the ambiguity of saying an abbot "has the place of Christ" from the recent discussion on a conciliar text, "The Life and Ministry of Priests." Two bishops suggested that a priest's office was to be *alter Christus*. The objection was immediately raised that every Christian is an *alter Christus;* anyway, the phrase had never been used by the early Fathers of the Church. The suggestion was accordingly dropped and, from the same argument, we should stop thinking of the abbot as an *alter Christus*. The Rule makes it plain that Christ is everyone in the monastery: the sick, guests, the cellarer, lecturer, porter, and so on.

What my experience of reading and living the Rule suggests is that because the definition of an abbot as *alter Christus* is too vague, we must try to relate his role to *conversio,* but not just that of his brother. It must also include his own. This has led me to see the task of the abbot as follows:

1. His teaching should lead the monk to open his heart to God.
2. He must aim at a transformation of people and place, turning both monks and monastery into the house of God.
3. He must do all he can to ensure that this house of God is a house of compassion.

1. Helping Brothers and Sisters to Open Their Hearts to God

Primarily, an abbot is there to preach the gospel to his brothers, to help them see that God saves us only through the boundlessness of divine love. They already know that, but the abbot still has to repeat it ceaselessly or soon the thing everyone knows will be something everyone has forgotten or has even started to doubt. Since this is the gospel, the abbot won't find himself preaching it as his own personal opinion and discovery, and that will mean he can efface himself, hiding his ego behind the Word of God. All he needs to do is to make the Word audible and convincing. That Word alone, and not the abbot or abbess, is going to open the eyes of a hard heart to the light. No one is going to hear the Word unless it is proclaimed. So the first thing is for the abbot to be the slave of the Word. If he isn't, he risks becoming a mere administrator, worrying (as someone must) about those temporal concerns that Benedict wants him to delegate. Having delegated them, he is still going to find himself having to represent the community to any authorities outside the monastery with which it has dealings. Someone has to represent the monastery and someone qualified (that of course will usually mean the abbot), but I think we have discovered how much easier it is to represent the community outside the monastery than it is to present the Word to the community inside it. Yet unless an abbot is inspired by the Word to proclaim it, he is not going to inspire the monastery by taking part in its day-to-day life.

The decisive question God will ask an abbot is whether he has given the Word to his brothers. Only by responding to that Word is a monk going to seek, find, and return to God. Our return to God is the only reason the Word became flesh, and it is the only reason the abbot became abbot. One word can say it all: *obedience*—providing we don't shut our eyes to the deep mystery that the word "obedience" is meant to convey. Even if we don't go so far as to imagine (as has happened in the past) that obedience means training monks in the way we train horses for the circus, we must still never think of obedience as doing what we are told so as to make community life possible. Obedience doesn't even begin to exist until it is a free expression of our love. Making obedience possible isn't the chief function of an abbot. The return to the God of each and all in any community is the concern of each and all in that community. We can treat every event in the community as a Word of God to which we can respond. If you are beginning to ask how we can possibly obey so many different voices, that means you have begun to see what the true role of an abbot is. He is the one who must ensure that all these voices are heard as a symphony and that all its movements are played and obeyed in harmony. In a congregation as varied as this, some abbots use the traditional short daily chapter for teaching the community; others prefer to speak at greater length but at much greater intervals.

2. Helping the Community Become the House of God

Though the abbot can't delegate this task to others, he must try to share it with them and not try to run the monastery as if he were a householder running his own house. The Rule wants the monastery to be God's house, a place of justice and peace.

Because it is God's house, we can discover in what sense an abbot can be called the vicar of Christ by remembering that when David wanted to build a house for God he was told that God would build one for him. This is a truth that every community really should take to heart because it is the very foundation of our liberty, the one thing that gives the cellarer, the craftsmen, and all the officials the freedom they need to take appropriate initiatives. What it gives the abbot is freedom to exercise his overall responsibility. What it gives the monk is freedom to preserve the spirit of poverty. Perhaps you will let me take this opportunity to say that poverty has to include not just a lack of material possessions but also a lack of vocations. So many of our monasteries seem obsessed with the desire to be rich in numbers. Only recently a superior general was talking about this human weakness which, however understandable, can become a major threat. He was asking why we should assume that God gives a special blessing to a monastery just because it happens to have a large community. Do the rich serve God better than the poor?

To complete these remarks on the House of God, let me add something on the well-known phrase *ordinavit caritatem*. I find it the perfect summary of what an abbot's job is—to ensure that everyone has his task. Rather than giving commands, the abbot entrusts monks with their tasks and sends them with a mission to fulfill. Christ never gave commands to his friends, only to devils: "As the father sent me so I send you." To be entrusted with a mission means that one is allowed to fulfill it in freedom. That is quite different from having to carry out a command, and different again from receiving a mere permission. Permissions operate in rather obscure ways, while it is clear that to receive a mission is to be sent as an envoy; and this, indeed, is the root of all the Church's ministries. We can place the ministry of monks who receive their mission from the abbot parallel to the technical sense of an ordained minister. In French, one's "job" is one's *metier*, a word that comes from the Latin *ministerium*, ministry (with some influence from *mysterium*, mystery). [TRANSLATOR'S NOTE: In English, of course, we don't have this verbal link between a *minister* or assistant and his *metier*: his job, craft, occupation, trade, or business.] Nevertheless, we can see how every task is open to the same dignity that marks a strictly ecclesiastical ministry, providing only that that task is entrusted to one as a minister and that one has fulfilled it to the best of one's ability. *Ordinavit caritatem*: it needs a lot of love to bring about justice and peace, a lot of wisdom to bring about everything that that little phrase implies—only two words, but I am haunted by their melody.

3. The Abbot and Compassion

We don't expect the abbot to carry out in person the job of doorkeeper, refectorian, cook, infirmarian, confessor, and lecturer; yet he has one specific responsibility that can't be shifted onto others, and that is to make sure that the poorest, the most unskilled, the least endowed, and the weakest are properly treated in the community.

To actually be with them all the time or even to remember them all the time wouldn't be possible. You don't have the time, for one thing, and you would need "to let this mind of Christ be in you," and few of us possess such treasures. All of our monasteries, however, can show a good record of making such monks feel at home, giving them all the help and advice they need, so it hardly seems necessary for me to elaborate the point except to point out that compassion isn't feeling sorry for someone but helping members to discover inner abilities, an inner resource, that will help them become helpful to those who in that respect are poorer than they.

Looking back over so many centuries of monastic history can make it hard to understand the attitudes and personalities of some notable abbots and abbesses of the past. Among them are some that seem to us quite eccentric and weird—and yet they seem to have been accepted by the monks and nuns who were their contemporaries. Heaven knows what monks and nuns in two or three centuries' time will make of the superiors contemporary with us today. Still, it doesn't seem to me that I have been caricaturing what St. Benedict tells us about the sort of person an abbot should be. At least I hope I haven't done that in my attempt to show him as an evangelizer, as entrusting each monk with a task that by helping the whole community return to God will help the whole human race return to God—a witness to divine compassion. In his *Essays on Evangelization,* Fr. Arrupe hopes that a superior, even if he lacks all the normal requirements, will at least be a person of compassion; and that, as I see it, is exactly what St. Benedict hoped too.

INTRODUCTION TO PART II

Part II is going to be about the proper way of using an abbot, using a person of compassion as a tool; but by way of introduction, let me insert a few reflections on a question one of you asked about the abbot's council. From my own experience I can say that this is one more of those difficult problems that would be wrong to avoid. From monastery to monastery and even from abbot to abbot in each community, there seem to be no hard and fast rules about how often the council should meet or what they should discuss. Some meet every month, some every two months, some once a year; others let more than a year elapse between meetings unless one becomes necessary under canon law. In some cases the councils discuss all the routine affairs of the monastery; in others they discuss long-range policies in only the broadest terms; then there are the cases where a meeting is held because the abbot wants advice on some particular problem.

Being a sort of privy council, these discussions are not usually made public. Meeting in private, they can indeed get quite heated. A letter like this has to consider the norm, a monastery with a living tradition of openmindedness in which the concern of every monk is for others rather than for himself. Even in the ideal monastery an abbot's council could take many forms: it could be a meeting of brothers who, by listening to each other, try to see what the community is capable of, given its present limitations; or, equally, it could be a meeting concerned with the future, with some still distant goals to which the community can aspire. The question asked of me labeled one kind an "organ of discernment," the other an "organ of research." Either kind is possible, providing the Council of Deans is aware that by definition it is meeting in order to proffer advice to the abbot. It must also be aware that it cannot override or replace the chapter meeting where all those in final vows can fulfill their obligation to the community by helping it reach a decision.

Per se, the council has no decision-making role, and the advice it gives the abbot should have regard to those three aspects of the abbot's role that

I have spoken about in the first part of this letter. To do that properly means that all the members present must have total confidence in each other. If that mutual confidence is really unrestricted, then there can't be any restrictions on the ideas that are put forward, however Utopian; and so much the better if the monk putting them forward can do so with foresight and imagination, providing, of course, that he doesn't try to impose his ideas on the others.

The sort of monk any abbot would find helpful on his council will be someone who is both animated by faith and gifted with intelligence. Other than that, one can't lay down any regulations except to point out that the abbot and the members of his council have to learn to work together, and that this in itself can be a valuable form of education. One can't expect every member of the council to be equally helpful. On top of that, the council is a specialized form of tool and must be prepared to develop it's own particular methods. The way a group of seven or ten can work together won't be the same for groups of three or fifty. Perhaps if our abbots could discuss this among themselves, they could learn from each other by sharing their experiences.

PART II: HOW MONKS CAN FIND THE ABBOT USEFUL

In spite of being scattered over so many continents, in spite of all the obvious but superficial differences, communities in our congregation are all very much alike: we all face the same double journey in much the same way.

On the ordinary journey of life, your understanding of what an abbot is will change in the normal course of events and will be different at age twenty, thirty, fifty, and so on. As your understanding of what an abbot is develops, you have to adapt your relationship with him accordingly. Your own development teaches you what freedom in the spirit is, teaches you not to be astonished at all the new insights you acquire. The second journey follows the path of the gospel taken by all who want to be followers of Christ: to follow him means following the pattern of his life as we see it sketched out by Paul for the Christians of Philippi. From his eternal existence Christ lowered himself to the nothingness of the cross, and from that nothingness manifested himself as our Lord. The monk, not as Christ but as *alter Christus*, must also pass from one plenitude, through his nothingness, to a greater plenitude.

To say that a novice doesn't see the abbot in the same way that he will when he is a senior is to point out a typical change on the path of ordinary life. It is on the *other* journey that moments come when we face our inner nothingness, moments that can't be measured by the distance we have traveled through life. These are the moments when an abbot can be of real use to a monk, though neither can foretell when they will happen, since they are just as likely to come in old age, or in middle age, as in youth.

At the next meeting of masters and mistresses of novices, I hope to develop what I said about passing through our inner nothingness by showing its importance as a moment of grace, as what Benedict sees as the supreme moment in a monk's life, bringing with it the promise of his true life and showing what is meant by the saying that to lose one's life is to gain it. This is the moment when every illusion is seen for what it is, and this is the moment in a monk's life when his abbot could be of the greatest use to him, since *this is what an abbot is for* on the path that Christ has marked out for us.

In every relationship between monk and abbot, I have noticed that there are always the three elements of affection, fear, and freedom.

When I visited a charterhouse, the prior received me; and when we reached his door, he realized he had to explain why it should have so many flowers and things growing in pots outside. It turned out that he had just returned from a visitation and these potted gifts were a typical Carthusian greeting and sign of affection. A monk who doesn't feel the cold will give his firewood to one who does; a monk who gets things to grow easily will give cuttings to those who can't. These signs and tokens are embellishments of affection, of monastic affection, which is the extension of Benedict's injunction that monks love their abbot with humble and sincere affection, an extension of preferring Christ to all things, since through him our affection is wide enough to embrace everyone and doesn't get monopolized by abbots and abbesses.

Monastic affection, filial or fraternal, has often been feared and repressed, but it should be encouraged and, above all, encouraged to be authentic. Of course, like every desert, the monastic desert has its own forms of mirage; but as long as we are still waiting for the dawn, our desire for the infinite can't exclude the attractiveness of the finite. This obviously poses more of a threat to the rigorists in any community, but we have to remember the full meaning of Christ's new and disturbing commandment to "love one another (as I have loved you)," that is, to the death of self, which makes it the most purifying of all the commandments.

In 1986, a Carthusian wrote:

> God gives himself to everything that is other than self, to everything that can be reached by my love, and until I become a self-giving creature I am not yet ready to give myself to God. Everything that is other than myself lies between God and myself because it is necessarily in God and in myself. The only way of escaping from the level of mere appearances is to accept the other as other than myself. But to accept the other as other means that first I must accept my own loneliness, my own narrowness and dependence, and then I can accept everyone who is other, with all

his limitations and faults and shortsightedness. What I can accept, then, isn't only his presence in my heart and in its silence and recollection, because then I shall be able to accept my own need to accept the absoluteness of my dependence, the absolute contingency of my existence. I shall be able, then, to accept my own need to accept the presence of everything and anything that I find boring, upsetting, and disturbing; especially if it separates me from my own interior image of God. We have to depend totally on God's will for the fact that we exist at all, it is his will that we should accept all the limitations imposed by our existence. Affection for the other doesn't depend on what we feel for him, but on the giving of ourself. (*Einsam und Gemeinsam: La Vie Spirituelle* 671.555ff.)

Fear is known and understood by everyone. Even the abbot can be afraid of his community, especially if he thinks of it as "his" community rather than Christ's. When a monk, on the other hand, feels afraid of his abbot, it is in most cases either because the "authority" of the abbot has presented itself as something impersonal or because it has been reduced to the level of "having the last word." In that sort of situation a monk isn't likely to consider his abbot an obvious tool in the work of *conversio*. Considering how large our congregation is, I find it encouraging to realize how rare it is to find an awkward situation like this blowing up dramatically. On the whole, I would say that monks and nuns are only too aware of the fact that fear has always been the devil's trump card. Just being aware of that is enough to stop him playing it.

Fear is a weed. One way to uproot it is to admit what things make us afraid and, better still, to admit it to the person who makes us afraid. That is a decisive step into spiritual freedom. The proper relationship between a monk and his abbot depends on freedom. Liberty always comes to us directly from God, and the whole purpose of a monk having an abbot is frustrated without it. Everything Christ has revealed concerns freedom, and progress in becoming free is progress in the monastic life. That is why it can't be hurried—freedom isn't something that comes automatically—it is offered by God, but we have to accept it and we all (including myself) need real courage to accept it.

Conclusion

Let me summarize this letter by composing a short dialogue between the young monk (M1) whose mind has not yet been pacified and a senior monk (M2) who has attained inner peace. They are discussing their abbot, and the young monk who is still disturbed begins the conversation:

M1: The abbot's conferences never seem to say enough.
M2: Tell him to give them more frequently.
M1: What would he say? He might just go on and on.
M2: Ask him to speak to you privately, heart to heart.

M1: He doesn't know my heart.

M2: Then open it for him.

M1: I'm afraid of him telling the others.

M2: Then tell him that that is what you are afraid of—or are you just afraid it was you he was getting at in the last conference? I don't think he meant anybody in particular. After a silence he adds: The more you ask the more you receive. Superiors always have their own *conversio* to think about as well as ours. If you think of *conversio* as something each individual has to work at, then it wouldn't make any difference if they gave their conferences to a brick wall instead of to you. *Conversio* has to be *personal,* but that isn't the same as *individual.* Individuals become persons only when they relate to each other. If you bolt the doors and block the windows, there is a good chance that you are going to damage yourself. Still at peace with himself, the *senex* got up and went off. The next time he saw the abbot he said, "What about opening a few windows?"

As for the abbots and abbesses, what words can I find to put into their mouths? As their days draw to a close, shouldn't they find it in them to say: Lord let me now depart in peace, for mine eyes have seen your salvation in those whom you confided to me?

Denis Huerre, *Abbot-president*
Congregation of Subiaco
Sant' Ambrogio, Rome

Love and "Conversio"

Dear Brothers and Sisters,

You must not be surprised by the heading of this letter, for Pentecost in the New Testament is a day of fire and violent wind. It was a day that we see as decisive in the life of the Church and the *conversio* of the world, a fecund and abiding moment in Christianity when *conversio* toward the Source and the spreading of love on earth go hand in hand, inseparably.

However, it is a fact that some will feel irritated when we talk of love, as if that were all there is to talk about; in 1930 a certain abbot was denounced during a canonical visitation for always having this one word on his lips. Some religious who thought they were on earth to suffer saw in the use of this word a certain provocation, a psychological and spiritual illusion. I happen to think that, on the contrary, we never speak enough of love, since love is our very life. But it is not easy to talk continually of love, and I confess it is with a certain amount of trepidation that I have chosen the theme of love and *the conversio* of the monk. I dare do so because I have had occasion to see for myself that not one of you, monks and moniales, is afraid to face up to the questions raised by the reality of love and the difficulty of *conversio*. As if love were already a given, and *conversio* uncertain.

Love expresses itself spontaneously—at least for a Christian—in two affirmations, both of which give a prominent place to the verb *to be*. The first affirmation is: You are. The second one is: I am with you.

When I say "you are," I am in fact making a personal discovery of primordial importance: there are others besides myself. What takes place, then, is a certain going-out-of-myself, a real birth of my true self. It is an act of adoration or admiration, depending on who it is that I say "you are" to. Whether my admiration is for someone that I can see (*mirari* means to look at) or my adoration is for the One, God, whom I cannot see but can only praise with my lips (*os,* mouth); no matter whether I use my eyes or my lips, it is from my deepest self that I exclaim: You are.

And when I say "I am with you," I go forward yet another step; I am not just in front of you or against you, but I am with you, which translates readily into: I am, through you and for you.

These two statements, "you are," and "I am with you," are declarations of love. They may not express all there is to say about love—for love in and of itself cannot say everything—but they do at least, better than many other statements, express the permanence of love, when they are said to a being who remains with us.

Can we, monks and moniales, aspire to absolute love, or should we on the contrary be content with rare experiences of love? I realize, as I write these words, that each of you has had differing personal experiences of love—as many different ones as there are of you. I also well know that the paths that have led to your monastic profession are widely divergent. Some of you have had much love in your lives while others have enjoyed little true family life. The experience of adolescence, as well, varies greatly from one person to the next; and friendship itself, such a positive force, has many different faces. Some of you have been engaged to be married or have been married. We must draw on all of this valuable human capital and not leave it aside, let alone denigrate it. What does love mean, in fact, for the monk and the moniale?

In point of fact, all the preceding letters I have sent you were all about love, whether I wrote about *lectio divina,* stability, beauty, old age, desire, the liturgy, the abbot, or other aspects of the gradual *conversio* of the monk. Yet in this last letter, devoted like the others to monastic *conversio,* I should like to emphasize the reality of love.

This letter will consist of two parts: the first will speak of St. Benedict as educator who introduces the monk to the love of the Trinity. The second part will address contemporary questions that are, in fact, eternal as well.

1. Benedictine Introduction to the Love of the Trinity

Let us begin with what is a specifically Christian innovation. When we expressed love using the phrases "you are" and "I am with you," these were words used by many people who do not consider themselves Christian. We must find more to say, and this brings us straight to the heart of the specifically Christian revelations on the subject of love: on the one hand, our God is one God, but in three Persons, and on the other hand, all of humanity is one in Christ. From these truths we see that it is God and human beings who will express their love in an entirely new way. From this point on there will be a continual going back and forth from the singular to the plural and from the plural back to the singular, and this movement adds new and unexpected resonance to our two statements of love, "you are" and "I am with you." Even though a baptized person and a non-baptized person can say these same words, they do in reality express now a different way of looking at the person to whom we address them.

The Trinity of Christianity is not a breaking up of the one God, and the one-ness of humanity brought about in Christ does not mean that the individuality of each person is somehow wiped out. But we know from our experiences of Christmas and Pentecost that everything is intertwined: every single reality has a Trinitarian aspect of plenitude that ultimately is the foundation of its individuality. In every individual loving action, no matter how brief it may be, the three divine Persons as well as all other human beings are always present. A somewhat vulgar expression in contemporary French slang calls loving "bursting." We might rather say that loving means always to have some presentiment of, or even the full experience of, a certain going-beyond-oneself, perhaps even the experience of plenitude.

How does St. Benedict go about introducing the novice to this Christian art where the actors are at one and the same time the Holy Trinity, all of humanity, and one's own self? The Rule, which assuredly is not a dogmatic treatise, could nevertheless be justifiably called The Art of Loving—which goes much further than any science of love.

St. Benedict's teaching, it seems to me, comes to us in two forms: firstly, by relating the professed monk or moniale clearly to each Person of the Trinity; and secondly, by a pedagogy whose sacramental character I would like to emphasize.

The Professed in His or Her Relationship with Each of the Divine Persons

From the very beginning of the Rule, God and humans are seen to be gazing longingly at each other, which is a perfect definition of love as personal and mutual desire.

We do not see in God the caring and patient Father, the sort of paternalism that we abhor in human behavior, full of sentimentality and self-serving, operating at a distance. This kind of fathering evokes infantilism and childishness, and we must reject it. Quite the contrary, the fatherhood of God is expressed as an empowering of consciousness, the consciousness of personal freedom of response—that is, of responsibility. To be a son or daughter of God is to be reborn again and again, which obviously is not possible in terms of human birth. This contrast stands out sharply in John's use (1 John 3:9) of the vocabulary of human regeneration in writing about our birth as sons of God: we are born of an abiding seed that is ever active in us.

The relationship between the professed religious and Christ can be summed up in a word: Christ will always be the preferred One because of what is said of him in the New Testament: he is the unique One of God. And he must become the unique One for each of us, the One we prefer above all else.

Human beings, generally speaking, tend not to expose the preferences of their hearts. If everyone knew them, they would quickly incur all sorts of complications that could prevent love from bearing fruit. Whereas in reality love is by nature fecund: it is the freedom to give of oneself and to receive the freely given gift of the other.

The only preference of love that can be truly proclaimed is the preference for Christ. When absolute choice is totally authentic, it reveals its true nature as the source and origin of all other loves and affections. While there are of course loves that are mere passing fancies of the heart, the choice of Christ above all others is lasting, founded on invincible hope.

At this point I like to think of Père Abbot Placide, who died some thirty-six years ago. Although he had led what appeared to us to be a perfect and even exemplary life, he went through the harrowing experience of believing himself rejected by God; his close friend Marthe Robin had the same experience. When we grasp how awful this must have been, his words repeated on his deathbed over and over, "Christ is everything," have all the more impact on us; these words were his legacy to us and were engraved on his headstone.

The relationship of the professed to the Holy Spirit is inevitably a matter of some subtlety. As we read through the pages of the Rule, we read of the growth in *dilectatio,* of the purification of the heart, the progress from fear to love, the capacity for true discernment of the better and wiser choice, the *discretio* of truth in obedience to God. Beyond the realities of human weaknesses (and cenobitic life certainly has its picturesque moments!) we read of the pleasantness of human relationships made possible by the attainment of virtue and spiritual awareness. It would be easy to read in the Rule the practical application of the promises of the gospel relative to the Holy Spirit who is: consoler, revealer, inspirer, constant and discreet presence—in a word, love.

This cursory review of the close relatiosnhip between the divine Persons and the Christian monk demands the immediate mention of his relationship with his fellows, within this small portion of humanity represented by his monastic community. Who among us is not aware of the absolute necessity of testing our love of God by weighing against it our love of our brethren? But each and every one of us has had occasion to speak of this principle with guests or at some conference or other, and I don't pretend to have anything new to teach you on the subject. But I would like to share with you my thoughts on the pedagogy of St. Benedict.

Monastic Pedagogy: the "Conversio" to Love

Because the life of the monk is localized and limited, it is in danger of being thought insignificant. For this reason we need to keep in mind the power of *conversio* to open the heart to love.

I will now be setting out into territory that may come as a surprise to you: and that is the sacramental life of the Christian. It is well known that

St. Benedict (and after him St. Bernard and St. John of the Cross) has little to say about the sacraments. Still, the sacraments had at that time the same function as they do ever and everywhere: to make it possible for a human life to meld into the divine, on earth as in heaven, precisely through the harmonization of separate wills—"What you want, I want"—which is the whole of love. Despite this silence of St. Benedict on the concrete use of the sacraments, I see in the sacramental life of the Christian the essentials of monastic pedagogy, especially in the case of the primary sacraments of baptism and the Eucharist.

Baptism—or rather the pedagogy leading up to baptism—seems to me to have informed the development of monastic pedagogy. We must also be careful to see St. Benedict as he saw himself, as someone who was bringing in something new, an initiator. His Rule is just that, an initiation, and to the degree that it is progressive—and therefore profound—it is a wellspring that one can draw from throughout life with all its surprises.

Let us compare the three points at which the Rule speaks of bringing someone into the community—or of bringing someone back into the community—namely, the welcoming of a novice, the welcoming of a guest, and the welcoming back of a brother who may have been under provisional excommunication due to a momentary spiritual lapse. In each instance I find the same formula, in fact the very same progression of Christian conversion being carried out in love: putting the word of God into practice—frequent readings of the Rule to the novice; verses of the Bible to the guest almost as soon as he has arrived; a spiritual talk with the "sympect" (a mature and wise monk) who is capable of persuading even the most obdurate of monks. And examination of faith as well—above all, faith in the divinity of Christ (the rule is anti-Arian), because if one does not believe in Christ the Lord, what sort of conversion would he be seeking? Finally, there is an examination of the personal life of the novice, the guest or the returned monk, because it is never enough for a person to know his lesson—he must put into actual practice the teaching of God. At the end comes the invitation to the kiss of peace and integration into the community, each to his appropriate place.

Am I wrong to see in all this the constant structure of the catechumenate in Christianity? For such it seems to be: communication of the word of God—for it alone reveals the depths of the heart and brings about what only the divine can do, the *conversio* of this human being into the son of God in Christ; the examination of faith (the famous baptismal scrutinies) and its translation into personal conduct; acceptance of the newcomer into the community with his or her naming as brother or sister (formerly a part of baptism, and still done in religious life today); and lastly, faithful efforts to do everything possible to assure the return of anyone who must at some time leave or be absent for a while.

The Eucharist is the perfect experience of re-integration, not only the actual liturgical Eucharist that St. Benedict scarcely mentions but also the Eucharist in the widest possible sense, the Eucharist as life itself as suggested in the Rule in two references that to my mind are luminous with meaning.

First there is the provision that the chart given to the professed, and which represents him or her entirely, should be wrapped up in the same cloth as the bread and wine prepared for the Eucharistic sacrifice. As in the case of these ritual oblations, he or she is also going to be transformed. This little detail has the force of a true symbol and contains in itself the future of the monk or moniale: he or she is to become Eucharist also, praise of God and a gift of self, a spiritual sacrifice for the salvation of the world. Yes, no less than that.

The second reference to the Eucharist lies in the prescription that the professed must not only be Eucharist but must also enact the Eucharist in everything he or she does. This is my understanding of St. Benedict's respect for things as well as people: if the chalice is to be respected, it is not for its style, its age, the material—gold, silver, pottery or crystal—of which it is made, but for its closeness to the Blood of Christ and its closeness to ourselves, for without it, how could we partake of the Blood of unity? And all other objects have this proximity, not with the Body and Blood of Christ but with what the consecrated species symbolize: the kingdom of God that has arrived among us.

We could continue at some length with these suggestive references of St. Benedict, for whom absolutely everything is part of the kingdom. I have on three or four occasions celebrated Mass in an airplane. A Mass over the world? Others have already written, and better than I could, about the cosmic role of the Eucharist. Certainly the Rule of St. Benedict's Rule in all its sobriety leads us to think along these lines; and indeed it is no far-fetched interpretation, for surely a human being made of flesh and spirit is a microcosm of the entire world, inspiring us to praise of God and leading us to reflect about the *conversio* of man.

Used as we are to these admittedly sublime Christian perspectives, we nevertheless remain well aware of the obvious gap between what we are able to realize in our everyday existence and these glimpses of dazzling spiritual reality. For this reason we do well not to offer ouselves as a model for anyone, and it behooves us to reflect on some particular ticklish situations. These will make up the second part of my discussion.

2. A Few Contemporary—and Eternal—Questions

It is not my intention here to catalog our problems and obstacles, but rather to offer as material for reflection for individuals as well as communities certain subjects that are both old and new—because they are dynamic.

Totality and Infinity

You may recognize this heading as the title of a book that has made its author, Emmanuel Lévinas, famous throughout the world. I don't pretend to have understood everything this philosopher has written, but I have found in his work some insights relative to my subject, love and *conversio*. When we speak of one or the other, should we use the concepts of totality or of infinity?

Like everyone else, I have noticed how rarely St. Benedict uses the term *perfect*. This is undoubtedly due to the fact that even when he promises the novice and above all the professed that he will realize his utmost desire (you will reach these heights of perfection), St. Benedict knows that such an attainment cannot be reached by human will alone, but that it depends on the will of God both for its impetus and its achievement, with God working deep within the human being and engaging his cooperation.

Perhaps he foresaw, as he had already seen in his own time, the excesses of all those "perfect ones" who were to arise one after the other, century upon century, and in all religions, including Christianity, and he rejected as non-Christian every form of totalitarianism. For monastic life could certainly be prone to totalitarianism either in its authority (the Rule says "tyranny") or in timid submission (which the Rule calls sterile and false obedience). There is also a danger of totalitarianism in some ascetic programs (rigid training), as there is also in the tyranny of the past for some people or of the future for others. But we are well-acquainted with the avatars of monastic history, and we know the measures we must ever take to avoid the danger of totalitarianism in our lives.

It is the infinite that must be the object of our desire, that which is limitless, without boundaries. It is the Invisible, the Unknowable, that we must seek gropingly; it is the unfathomable mystery of Christ that is the object of faith, and it is the inexhaustible wealth of Scripture that we must meditate upon.

But there is a paradox to all this: the more our Christian faith is turned towards the infinite and the limitless, the greater value it sets upon our lives and our very limited acts. But whereas totalitarianism progresses through accumulation and adding on, the infinite progresses by means of a permanent *conversio,* one could even say transfiguration and diffusion. Totalitarianism piles up limitations, while the infinite takes note of them only to make them permeable to something new: the presence of the other. For the other is without limit in the case of God; in the case of a person, the limitations are different from mine and can make me more complete and reveal me to myself as a desiring being. Clearly, when we speak of love and *conversio*, it is not totality that is at work but infinity.

But what is the import of all this for our structured monastic life?

The Value of Structures

If we look at the meaning of the word itself, the value of structures is that they construct the human being, and everyone is in agreement on this. But the danger of structures when they are poorly applied is that they can inhibit growth, stunting human beings instead of helping them grow according to the Christian and Pauline ideal.

So we have a permanent problem with structures, more than other people do. Should we multiply our observances or reduce their number? How do we know what is the right amount that nourishes life in the truth? This is up to the individual communities, who are all well-aware of what is spiritually at stake in the answer they bring to these questions.

Without going into specific answers to this question, I would like to cast a little light at this point on the subject of structure. *Autonomy* is a word we like as a synonym of maturity, of the capacity to respond in a personal way to the call of God. But basing ourselves on biblical revelation, as well as on the contributions of the social sciences to our understanding of the development of the human being and of entire peoples, we categorically reject the notion of independence.

Not depending on others leads to death rather than to life, and it is an illusion held unfortunately by many individuals, as well as collectivities, that total independence is a possibility. As far as monastic communities are concerned, the norm is autonomy, not independence. Or else we see an unfortunate lapsing into sectarianism, which is something that unfortunately has always been a danger.

Let me share a second thought on structures: they are indispensable for true self-knowledge, both for individuals and for communities. When the structures are authentic, they reveal, as nothing else can, the possibilities as well as the limitations of the person and the group. The work of *conversio* and love is made all the easier. But this is particularly true when the ambiguity mentioned above is avoided: it is not the structure that converts the monk, it is God. We have all had occasion to notice how salutary it can be to get rid of some particular structure. An example is the breaking up of the Twelve on Holy Thursday and Good Friday: the disciples were dispersed, and this was necessary for the manifestation of the Church as the creation of Christ and Christ alone in and through his victory over death, and not as the work of the consensus of men.

There are many lessons for us indeed in this fundamental episode in the life of the Church. If some of our monastic structures are not directly inspired by the Gospels (and our best safeguard is the Church's approval of our constitutions), they would be as fragile as many worldly structures and might perhaps exhibit their pitiless harshness as well. Herein lies that danger of totalitarianism we discussed above.

Monastic Celibacy

It seems that we did not get around to talking about celibacy except in terms of its spirituality—which we did very well—until a considerable number of professed had left monastic life to get married: and now we are addressing the issue in terms of its reality for the whole human person. It is a human reality that manifests itself in myriad ways, one of which is sexuality, which none would deny is a given of human life, both hidden and open to view, which is not absent from the way a man looks at a woman or a woman looks at a man, unless of course some misogyny or misanthropy is at work.

While it is natural to maintain a certain reserve in speaking of human sexuality, a reserve that is in keeping with such a deep reality, it is nonetheless encouraging to see that monastic communities have broken their habitual silence on the subject of the voluntary celibacy of the monk or moniale. The question has been raised as to whether it is enough for the religious to have chosen celibacy, in order to live it well and in the light of day. And the obvious answer has shown itself to be no.

I will not go into this topic at any length, as it is up to the individual communities to approach it and find their own way of handling it, but I would like to mention the conclusion reached by a certain religious (who was not a monk) who helped a lot of married Christians, as well as religious men and women. He finds that beyond any doubt married life is more difficult than celibacy, with the caveat that this latter state contains more perils, in that it is the subject of many more illusions. I might add here that a truly fraternal community life, as opposed to mere common life, can greatly help the celibate to avoid these difficulties, but only so long as he or she accepts as normal for the monastic state the practice of constantly forgetting oneself and not giving into the temptation to live just for oneself in order to better cultivate one's garden.

3. Conclusion

It is possible—and necessary—to finish a letter, but the work of *conversio* and love is never finished. In ending my letter and my meetings with you, I would like to risk asking another question: was St. Benedict a mystical writer or not?

Around 1955 a young girl who had numerous degrees and professional experience announced to Abbot Journet that she had decided to enter a monastery. Now Father Journet objected that, humanly speaking, she could be of much more use somewhere else. But when the girl insisted, this friend of Benedictines, Cistercians, and Carthusians concluded: "Then enter, but never stop reading the mystics." Did he perhaps say this to her because he foresaw that any life, monastic or not, is threatened by dullness, busyness, and even discouragement from overwork; it can be threatened as well by the need to distract oneself from all this heaviness? The future cardinal who was neither a dreamer nor a dilettante surely intended with this piece of advice to express the primordial importance of the hidden face of things, in life and especially in religion. When I visited the cloister of Val-Sainte, where he is buried in the Carthusian way, with nothing written on his head-stone, not even his name, I wondered why this is done; it seemed to me then that our true name is a hidden name, given by God alone, who gives our poor little human glory the grace of being transfigured into his own divine glory.

Does St. Benedict say anything more? His Rule is the book of our mys-tical life, and it contains the essentials of the gospel, which is the book of mysticism par excellence. And I read in the rule a number of ideas that I have found also in my reading of those authors who are widely recognized as mystics. Let me mention just three of these.

Nicholas of Cusa, a Church figure at the time of the councils of Pisa, Constance, and Basel—which says it all—was a man of action and decision in the physical and mechanical sciences, a theologian, and a mystical au-thor absorbed by the gaze of God. He was a man of contrasts who wrote, not surprisingly, a famous work that defended his principle of the *coinciden-tia oppositorum* called *De Docta Ignorantia* (1440). And I find, as I try to live by his Rule, that St. Benedict was a master of this spiritual art of harmoniz-ing these two fundamental aspects of Christian life, the human and the di-vine. To truly live this contrast is to be a Christian, and our lives acquire thereby the essential face of mysticism.

As for St. John of the Cross, I feel right at home when he says that in seeking God we will find him in the world and in the cosmos, and when he speaks of the true self that we receive from God alone. Benedict says the same thing, refusing to exclude any reality at all as a place of encounter with God for the monk, so long as he renounces his false self (Benedict says, "his own will") and receives himself, his true self, from God.

Listen to what St. John says: "How should I possess you, you who are in everything? How shall you give yourself to me, if you have not given me as well the heavens and the earth and all that are found therein? But above all, how shall you give yourself to me if you have not given me to myself?"

And I am equally comfortable with William of St. Thierry, which is natural, when he writes: "Let every man do his honest best in accomplish-ing for God what he can as a man. Even if he incurs calumny, God in his mercy will render his poor one justice and will take up his cause, because he did what was humanly possible for him to do."

Our human life and our divine life are forever intertwined. The mysti-cal life is a mysterious life. And *conversio* is not just a matter for the intellect (one might say of ideology) but a *conversio* of love and understanding, not human understanding of the divine, but the understanding between the I and the thou, of the being that I am among so many other beings and the Being that you are, my God and our God.

This letter has been a little long, but it is the last one. And so, let me say as we do in my native Provence—*à Dieu* (until God!)

Denis Huerre, *Abbot-president*
Congregation of Subiaco
Sant' Ambrogio, Rome